ULTIMATE cake

ULTIMATE
cake

BARBARA MAHER
Photography by Dave King

TED SMART

A DORLING KINDERSLEY BOOK

Project Editor
Debbie Major

Editor
Kate Scott

Senior Editor
Carolyn Ryden

Art Editor
Jo Grey

Designer
Emy Manby

DTP Designer
Karen Ruane

Managing Editor
Susannah Marriott

Senior Managing Art Editor
Carole Ash

Recipe Consultant
Val Barrett

Home Economists
Janice Murfitt
Angela Kingsbury

Production Manager
Maryann Rogers

First published in Great Britain in 1996 by Dorling Kindersley Limited
80 Strand, London WC2R 0RL
Reprinted 1996

First published as a Dorling Kindersley paperback 1998

This edition produced for The Book People Ltd
Hall Wood Avenue, Haydock, StHelens, WA11 9UL

A CIP catalogue record for this book is available from the British Library

ISBN 0 7513 0562 6

Reproduced in Italy by GRB Editrice, Verona
Printed and bound in Singapore by Star Standard Industries (Pte.) Ltd.

Contents

Introduction 6

A Gallery of Cakes 10

*A selection of some of the world's
most mouthwatering, tempting and spectacular
cakes, shown whole and in slices to reveal
their delicious fillings.*

Baking Essentials 30

A full-colour introduction to the key ingredients and equipment used in cake-making, with a photographic guide to the basic techniques and principles of baking.

Icings, Fillings & Decorations 138

Illustrated easy-to-follow instructions show how to achieve a professional finish with recipes for all the essential decorations, fillings and toppings.

Recipes 58

Over 100 recipes for cakes to suit every occasion, with detailed step-by-step instructions and additional information on advance preparation, freezing and storage.

Introduction

This is a book to savour. The cakes look good and taste even better. They are combinations of the best ingredients and the finest flavours – butter, eggs, flours, sugars, fresh and dried fruits, nuts, spices and aromatics. It is almost a history book, for it brings together classic cake recipes from countries as far afield as Italy, America and Japan, many with origins deep in the past. The different baking methods, influenced by itinerant travellers, immigrants, traders and invaders, reflect the culture, folklore and art of each nation's people throughout the centuries. And this diversity is still apparent today, for wherever one travels, one will find local specialities. As George Lang says in *The Cuisine of Hungary*, "Sachertorte is best in Vienna, Dobos is the finest in Budapest, cheesecake richest in New York", and recipes for all these cakes are included in the book.

The Origins of Cakes

The first cakes were made from simple ingredients as symbols of the mythical and magical superstitions of ancient religions. Early trading routes brought exotic spices north from the Far East; nuts, perfumed flower waters, citrus fruit, dates and figs from the Middle East; sugar cane from the Orient and South. During the Dark Ages in Europe the availability of these coveted ingredients was limited to monks and the wealthy aristocracy, who created cakes such as ginger and honey breads and biscuits baked flat and hard. In time, an increase in trading brought

A 17th-century cake mould

about a complete transformation in the eating habits of the western world. Arab traders and soldiers returning from the Crusades spread the use of spices and Middle Eastern-style recipes. In the principal trading towns of Middle Europe, guilds of specialist bakers were formed, and by the late Middle Ages spices were being used extensively in wealthier households all over Europe, inspiring skilful and more imaginative baking. As nuts and sugar became popular, so did "marchepane" – marzipan baked in embossed and carved wooden moulds depicting religious teachings.

Cakes for Special Occasions

The most important and luxurious cakes were baked for religious
festivals. They combined local dairy produce and ingredients
that grew abundantly in the surrounding countryside with
expensive, imported goods, such as nuts and spices.
Late-autumn cakes especially were cherished for their
long-keeping qualities through the winter months.
Over the years these cakes became traditional and
we still bake them in the same way with identical
ingredients for our own celebrations.

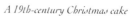

A 19th-century Christmas cake

The Emergence of a Café Society

An elaborate cuisine developed in the 16th- and 17th-century Italian
and French courts had, by the 18th century, become important in everyday
life too. Small pastry shops opened that grew into "cafés" and Vienna, with
the lavish lifestyle of the Habsburg court, a strong Turkish influence, and a
predilection for all things sweet, became the "Mother of Cafés". A book of
the time described a new confection as a "sumptuous cream-filled picture,
of eggs, sugar, butter, snow and a little flour". These sophisticated cakes, as
well as homely pastries, served with coffee and conversation became the
rage. *Kaffeeklatsch* (café society) had arrived in Central Europe.

Scene in a 19th-century French pâtisserie

Afternoon tea in a Victorian household

Tea-time

Afternoon tea appeared in late 19th-century Britain after the
Duchess of Bedford entertained friends with an elegant repast between
lunch and dinner. Plates of dainty sandwiches and cake-stands laden with
small, French-style fancy cakes were customary fare. Tea-tables were laid
with fine linen and costly silver or china tea-services, and pretty napkins
and silver forks were handed to each guest. As tea became cheaper it grew
in popularity, and tea-time became a ritual. In less wealthy homes "high-tea"
was served to the whole family at around six o'clock. Cold savouries and
homemade plain and fruited cakes were eaten with sweet, milky tea.

Baking Traditions in North America

In 17th-century America, Pennsylvanian Dutch settlers brought
with them wholesome cooking and delicious traditional baking, rich in
spices. These baked goods were sold at local markets, along with fresh
produce. By the early 20th century, "bake sales" and competitions at
agricultural fairs had become popular, as cooks tried to outdo even
the Viennese in their baking prowess. Cakes were now an essential feature
of the American table. Scandinavian settlers had brought with them a
tradition for drinking coffee and eating Danish pastries. Combined with the
fruity breakfast cakes, coffee and nut cakes, and doughnuts of Germanic
Europe, "Coffee klach" had found its way to the "New World".

The Role of the Written Word

Cookery books have also played a major part in spreading the
influence of different ethnic baking traditions. The writings in early
Arabic texts, the manuscripts of grand court kitchens, the scripts of humble
monks, guildsmen, master chefs and even of the ordinary housewife have
crossed continents, been copied and translated into many languages.
The last 150 years have seen the swiftest and
greatest cultural exchanges.

It is from those early cookery books that my own fascination
for baking has grown. For this book I have chosen a wide selection of
delicious recipes that are typical of their lands and traditional origins: from
simple butter cakes and light sponges filled with whipped cream
and brimming with ripe berries, to small crisp or chewy biscuits to serve
with dessert, and grand confections suitable for the finest banquet.
You will also find wickedly rich chocolate marvels finished with truffles,
appealing children's party cakes decorated with sweets, and elegant,
yet easy-to-make, flower-topped wedding cakes. In all, there are
more than 100 recipes to tempt and indulge you. I do hope that they will
give you as much pleasure as they have given me.

Points to Remember for Successful Baking

Baking is a skill for which the maxim "Practice makes perfect"
really does hold true. In this book you will find many detailed, step-by-step
photographs of the basic techniques, and practical tips designed to help you
achieve delicious and good-looking cakes. However, there are a few
essential rules that should always be followed carefully.

* *Choose a time when you can work without
distraction or interruption.*

* *Be sure that you have all the ingredients
required for any recipe before you start.*

* *Always use ingredients at room temperature.*

* *Weigh out and prepare all the ingredients before
you start mixing.*

* *Follow the same units of measurement
throughout a recipe; use either metric or imperial,
but never a mixture of the two.*

* *The right baking tin is essential for a perfect
result. Measure across the top of the tin from one
inside wall to the other and disregard any other
measurement stamped on the base of the tin.*

* *The oven should be switched on before starting
preparation and have reached the recommended
baking temperature before use.*

* *The correct oven temperature is crucial for baking
success. For perfect accuracy, it is best to check the
temperature with an oven thermometer placed in the
centre of the oven before baking the cake.*

* *The baking times given in each recipe can only be
used as a guide because every oven varies. Check the
cake approximately 5 minutes before the end of the
baking time in the ways shown on page 50, then
remove or leave in the oven.*

* ***Warning: Raw eggs can transmit salmonella.
Avoid serving recipes with this warning to the
elderly, young children and pregnant women.***

A Gallery of Cakes

This mouthwatering collection of delicious cakes, illustrated in full-colour, gives a tempting glimpse of the many exciting recipes you will find in the book. There are cakes for all occasions, and whether you prefer a multi-layered creamy confection or a dark, rich chocolate sponge, a fresh fruit flan packed with juicy berries or an airy meringue, this inspiring guide will help you to make your choice.

Luxury Layered Cakes

Biscuit de Savoie (See page 65.)

Layered cakes were introduced to Britain and the United States by 19th-century immigrants from central Europe, who set up Continental-style pâtisserie shops to sell these luxurious confections. Exquisite blends of flavours and textures make layered cakes as much a feast for the mouth as for the eyes.

"A torte – is one with a pleasing appearance inside and out."

Confectioner's description, early 20th century

Caramel slices rest on chocolate cream rosettes

ESTERHAZY CREAM TORTE *is composed of two almond sponge layers filled with a potent cream made from wine and rum. Offer this at an elegant lunch party. (See page 71.)*

The sweet juices of fresh cherries permeate the sponge layers

SOUR CHERRY AND CHOCOLATE TORTE, *similar to Black Forest Kirschtorte. (See page 78.)*

Sponge layers are doused with rum and citrus-flavoured syrup

RUM AND CITRUS TORTE *is typical of torten popular in 19th-century Austria and Germany. (See page 73.)*

DOBOS TORTA *(above and left) is traditionally a confection of thin sponge layers, sandwiched together with a rich chocolate buttercream and covered with a clear sheet of caramel glaze. Here the caramel is cut into triangles and set in a fan design. (See page 74.)*

HAZELNUT MACAROON CAKE *improves in flavour as it matures. (See page 75.)*

Chocolate Cakes

Chocolate Chestnut Roulade

Chocolatl, a rich yet bitter drink, was valued as highly as gold by Montezuma II, king of the Aztecs. Columbus took the cocoa bean back to Spain in 1502 where it was kept secret for over 100 years. Eventually, in 1875 two Swiss chocolatiers created the first bar of milk chocolate, and so began the sweet revolution.

"From the fruit of the gods, the cocoa pod, comes the bean out of which cocoa powder and ten-pound chocolate bars are made."

Adrianne Marcus,
The Chocolate Bible (1979)

The ganache coating is made from chocolate and cream

CARACAS *is a delicious, sophisticated chocolate sponge, baked in an elegantly shaped Balmoral tin (see page 41) and covered with a rich chocolate ganache cream. (See page 84.)*

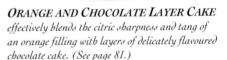

Orange mousseline buttercream makes a delicious filling and topping

ORANGE AND CHOCOLATE LAYER CAKE *effectively blends the citric sharpness and tang of an orange filling with layers of delicately flavoured chocolate cake. (See page 81.)*

A chestnut purée and dark rum filling complements the light sponge perfectly

CHOCOLATE CHESTNUT ROULADE *combines a moist sponge, full of chocolate and crunchy chopped nuts, and a filling of exquisite chestnut buttercream. (See page 82.)*

CHOCOLATE TRUFFLE TORTE *is a wonderful Swiss speciality with hints of spices and coffee. The chocolate sponge is moistened with syrupy spirits, sandwiched with whipped cream and a smooth chocolate buttercream, then finished off with wickedly tempting truffles laced with Tia Maria. (See page 80.)*

SACHER TORTE traditionally has no decoration other than its originator's name piped on to the highly glazed chocolate surface. I have done away with the writing and added a ring of chocolate leaves. (See page 85.)

Moist almond and chocolate sponge are encased in rich chocolate icing

Tia Maria adds a heady kick to the chocolate truffles

Cheesecakes

Italian Easter Cake

Traditionally served at Pentecost, cheesecake is often considered to be of Jewish origin, but it may be Italian in ancestry – the Ancient Romans are known to have eaten honey-flavoured cheese in savoury confections. Today it is enriched with eggs and cream, and enhanced with fruit, spices, or even chocolate.

"...the best way for these Cheesecakes is to make Coffynes in Patty-Pans, and fill them with the Meat near an Inch thick"

Richard Bradley, *The Country Housewife and Lady's Director* (1736)

ITALIAN EASTER CAKE *contains an unexpected filling of spiced ricotta cheese, cooked vermicelli pasta and finely chopped candied citrus peel. (See page 133.)*

Raisins soaked in dark rum add texture and flavour to the cheese filling

GOLDEN BAKED CHEESECAKE *is rich and yet perfectly light in texture, full of flavour and studded with raisins, just the way it should be. (See page 111.)*

Apricot jam helps bind the biscuit base together, giving it a slight crispness

MANGO AND PASSION FRUIT CHEESECAKE, *light and wonderfully fluffy in texture, is perfumed with fresh orange and passion fruit juice. (See page 109.)*

PASKHA *is reminiscent of delicious Italian cassata ice-cream. A combination of nuts, peel, raisins, cream and vanilla creates a rich and harmonious Russian Easter dessert. Use cream cheese instead of curd cheese for a richer flavour. (See page 131.)*

PECHE A LA MELBA CHEESECAKE
offers the sweet, delicate flavour of fresh
peaches in a simple cheese filling. Serve with
fresh raspberry sauce. (See page 110.)

Slightly sharp, fresh
raspberry sauce
transforms this into a
luxurious dessert

Slices of glacé fruit
arranged like jewels
on a Russian icon

Flans & Tarts

Tarte Tatin

A flan or tart is a simple, crisp container or "coffyne", as it was once known, with a filling. The filling is the attraction, and whether eye-catching circles of fruit, glistening syrupy, nutty mixtures, or tangy citrus custards oozing with baked aromatic juices, it is always designed to be irresistible.

"A tart…is but a kind of dinner plate…which may be eaten."

E.S. Dallas, *Kettner's Book of the Table* (1877)

Crème pâtissière prevents the fragrant fruit juices from soaking into the pastry

FRENCH FLAN WITH RED BERRIES *has both tart and sweet soft summer fruit packed tightly over crème pâtissière in a delicate pastry shell. (See page 91.)*

GLAZED FRESH ORANGE FLAN *makes a rich and striking dessert. The texture of the fruit, glazed with a tangy marmalade-like syrup, contrasts well with the smooth, buttery orange filling and crisp, short pastry. (See page 92.)*

Golden caramelized apples are baked under a crisp pastry crust

TARTE TATIN, *a warm upside-down apple tart, was created early in the 20th century by the Tatin sisters in France, and is said to be the result of a happy accident. (See page 95.)*

Shelled pecan nuts arranged over the top in concentric circles

PECAN AND MAPLE PIE *is a dream pie for anyone with a sweet tooth. It is splendidly dense, full of crunchy nuts and sticky with maple syrup. (See page 93.)*

Thinly sliced glazed
oranges create a
highly colourful,
shiny surface

Meringues

A pastry chef called Gasparini, who lived in Meiringen, Switzerland, was reputed to have created a composition of beaten egg whites and sugar in the 1720s. Affectionately known as "Meiringerli", these exceptionally light confections remain a speciality of the Bernese Oberland region but are popular everywhere.

"A jewel for the ladies... whose composition is as light and soft as whipped cream"

Antonin Carême, a famous 19th-century French chef

Simple meringues with cream

TORTA DI PINOLI *is made with lightly roasted pine nuts which give flavour and crunch to the meringue layers. (See page 115.)*

Thick layer of chocolate ganache

JAPONAIS *is a classic French combination. The meringue discs contain lightly roasted, crunchy hazelnuts, and are sandwiched with luxurious chocolate ganache. (See page 117.)*

SIMPLE MERINGUES *are sumptuous yet fragile creations, crisp on the outside and lightly aerated inside. Serve in pairs with whipped cream. (See page 112.)*

Decorated with fresh strawberries

Meringue batons are arranged over the top

MOCHA TRANCHE, *with its flavoured meringue and softly whipped cream, melts in the mouth, leaving the lingering warmth of chocolate and coffee. (See page 116.)*

SUMMER BERRY VACHERIN
makes a wonderful dessert for a
special occasion. Meringue discs are
layered with cream, flavoured with
liqueur and lightly crushed
raspberries and strawberries. The
spectacular confection is topped with
a mouthwatering display of fresh
summer fruit. (See page 114.)

Meringue is
layered with
raspberry and
strawberry cream

Tart fruit
contrast with the
sweet meringue

Fruit & Nut Cakes

Polish Coffee and Walnut Cake
(See page 103.)

Dried fruit and nuts are a classic combination. Chopped or ground nuts often replace butter and sometimes flour in a cake mixture because they are full of natural oils. They add subtle flavor and a distinctly rich and luxurious moistness to a cake, while fruit enhances the fragrance, deepens the texture, and improves the keeping quality of the cake.

" We were permitted only one piece of cake at tea-time, never two! To have two was considered greedy."

Michael Smith's Afternoon Tea
(1986)

Lemon glacé icing adds extra flavor

SPICED HONEY CAKE *is a wonderful winter cake, rich and moist. It is lightly spiced with cinnamon, ginger, and cloves and then decorated with glacé icing and crystallized ginger. (See page 98.)*

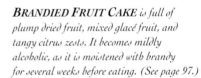

Some of the glacé fruit decoration should be served with each slice

BRANDIED FRUIT CAKE *is full of plump dried fruit, mixed glacé fruit, and tangy citrus zests. It becomes mildly alcoholic, as it is moistened with brandy for several weeks before eating. (See page 97.)*

Flaked almonds
dusted with
icing sugar

COCONUT LAYER CAKE, *a sweet and fluffy cake, is an American-style favourite. The slightly sharp tang of cranberry jelly complements the frosting of cream cheese and the fresh coconut coating. (See page 106.)*

SPANISH ALMOND SPONGE, *with its subtle taste of brandy or Grand Marnier and orange zest, is good to serve at tea-time, filled with plenty of whipped cream and crisp toasted almond flakes. (See page 107.)*

AMERICAN CARROT LOAF *is flavoured with grated carrot, chopped hazelnuts, orange zest and muscovado sugar, and topped with a light cream cheese frosting. (See page 89.)*

Marzipan carrots
denote the key
ingredient

Pastries & Biscuits

A selection of biscuits

Whether described as "petits fours", "biscuits de pâtisserie", "friandises", cakes or simply cookies, small edible temptations are offered in almost every country whenever richly roasted coffee and fine teas are served. They may be light and airy, or chewy and crunchy, and they are always hard to resist.

"To make Short cakes… your paste will be very short, therefore ye must make your cakes very little…"

The Good Huswives Handmaid (c. 1579)

A light dusting of icing sugar adds to the appeal

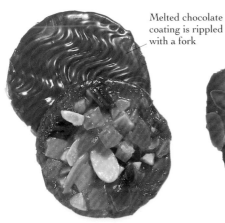

Melted chocolate coating is rippled with a fork

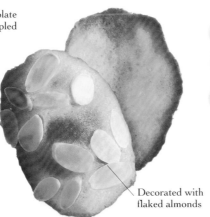

Decorated with flaked almonds

FLORENTINES *are made from colourful glacé fruit and flaked almonds, baked in a toffee-like mixture and coated with melted chocolate. (See page 119.)*

TUILES *gain their name from the curved French roof tiles they resemble. Wafer-thin and very crisp, they are good served with ice-cream desserts. (See page 120.)*

CHOCOLATE ECLAIRS, *the traditional small French pastries, are covered with plain chocolate and filled with a rich and creamy custard-like crème pâtissière. (See page 121.)*

FRUIT AND CREAM PUFFS *comprise crisp, golden domes of choux pastry filled to the brim with fresh soft fruit and lightly whipped cream. (See page 121.)*

A chocolate coating makes these biscuits hard to resist

Whipped cream can be flavoured with liqueurs

BUTTER BISCUITS *may be crisp to bite into but they have a soft centre. Traditionally the biscuits are piped into rings, scrolls or simple sticks and then dipped into melted plain chocolate. (See page 120.)*

SUGAR BISCUITS *are sweet, buttery and simple to make. Create different shapes by using decorative cutters, finish with a sprinkling of assorted coloured sugars and bake until crisp and golden. (See page 120.)*

Wedding Cakes

Croquembouche (See page 122.)

The rich and symbolic traditions of wedding cakes have developed over the centuries and remain with us today. Designed to be the centrepiece at a wedding feast and shared among the guests, the cakes are customarily multi-layered and sumptuously decorated.

"I sing of maypoles, hock-carts, wassails, wakes, Of bridegrooms, brides and of the bridal cakes."

Robert Herrick, *Hesperides* (1648)

Buttercream icing piped in a basket-weave pattern

Fresh flowers are pushed between the layers of cake

AMERICAN WEDDING CAKE *is made up of moist almond sponge layers flavoured with orange zest and chocolate, sandwiched together and decorated with orange buttercream. The fresh flowers arranged at the base of each cake tier add the finishing decorative touches. (See page 124.)*

Sugarpaste icing gives the cake a flawless finish

TRADITIONAL WEDDING CAKE *has two tiers of Baumkuchen and one of Traditional Plumb Cake covered in marzipan and then smooth, champagne-coloured sugarpaste. The whole cake is decorated with delicate sugar-frosted flowers. (See page 126.)*

Colour the sugarpaste to complement the shade of the flowers

Flowers are arranged in decorative cascades

Children's Party Cakes

Ribbon and Candle Cake

Every child loves to have a special birthday cake and here is a fantasia of ideas to mark the occasion. Designed to be fun to make as well as to look at, they also taste wonderful. Adapt the decorations to suit your own child's preferences and let your imagination run riot.

"He had a cake with icing on the top, and three candles, and his name in pink sugar…"

A. A. Milne, *Winnie the Pooh* (1926)

TEDDY BEAR CAKE *is ideal for young children with its light sponge and jolly decoration. Make extra parcels for the party guests as take-home gifts. (See page 136.)*

RIBBON AND CANDLE CAKE, *made from a deliciously moist carrot sponge, is covered with a soft cream cheese frosting and decorated with elegant candles and ribbons. (See page 137.)*

Brightly coloured icing hides layers of plain and chocolate sponge

The number of balloons matches the age of the child

Chocolate thins overlapped to make roof tiles

HEDGEHOG CAKE *with spikes of flaked chocolate and a sweet and fudgy chocolate cake centre covered with a rich chocolate icing.*
(See page 135.)

The face is shaped from marzipan

Chocolate spikes are pushed into the icing before it sets firm

Piped glacé icing window and door details

LITTLE HOUSES *are based on a simple Victoria Sandwich mixture, cut to shape and decorated in the style of traditional gingerbread.*
(See page 154.)

2

Baking Essentials

Learn the basic skills required
for baking from this clearly illustrated
step-by-step guide. Packed full of
useful hints and tips to ensure your
baking is trouble-free, it teaches the
key techniques from separating an
egg to checking a cake for readiness.
Basic recipes are provided for the
various types of pastry used in the
book. There is also a photographic
guide to the most useful kitchen tools
and all the essential bakeware, and
a visual catalogue of the best
ingredients to select for your pantry.

Basic Ingredients

Aim to keep a selection of these basic ingredients so that you may bake whenever you wish. The more unusual ones are available from healthfood stores. Your baking will taste delicious and look most appetizing if you choose only the best quality produce and the freshest dairy goods. Do not store any ingredients in large quantities as they soon deteriorate: it is better to keep smaller amounts and replace them more often.

Flours, Raising & Thickening Agents

The baking qualities of flours vary according to their ability to form gluten when moistened. Gluten sets when heated, trapping air in the mixture. The gluten in plain flour gives a soft texture; potato flour and cornflour produce very little, making a crumbly texture.

Plain and self-raising flour: *Plain flour is used on its own in whisked and rich fruit cakes and biscuits, or together with a raising agent. Self-raising flour already includes some baking powder.*

Rye flour: *A wholegrain brown flour which gives a rich colour and a delicious nutty taste to cakes and tea loaves.*

Potato flour: *Made from boiled, sieved and dried potatoes, this produces a delicate, airy cake.*

Semolina: *Fine-grained, rich in protein and starch, this gives a good texture.*

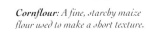

Cornflour: *A fine, starchy maize flour used to make a short texture.*

Gelatine: *Gives a taste-free, firm set to soft cake fillings and cheesecakes.*

Matzo meal: *Crushed crumbs of unleavened crackers used in place of flour and as a thickener.*

Bicarbonate of soda: *Acts as a raising agent when combined with an acid such as lemon juice.*

Baking powder: *This reacts with moisture to produce carbon dioxide, which helps a cake to rise.*

Cream of tartar: *An acidic substance that stabilizes egg whites during beating.*

Sweeteners

Sugars and syrups affect the structure of a cake and improve its texture, colour and flavour. Store in airtight containers in a cool, dry place.

Caster sugar: *Best for making whisked and creamed cakes, as the fine crystals dissolve and blend quickly with other ingredients.*

Golden syrup: *Gives the finished cake a moist texture.*

Honey: *Used for centuries, a natural sweetener enhancing the flavour and keeping quality of cakes.*

Maple syrup: *This sweetener has a strong, distinctive flavour.*

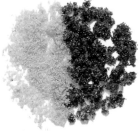

Icing sugar: *A fine, powdery sugar, ideal for icings and fillings. It must be sieved before use.*

Granulated and coloured sugars: *Use granulated in syrups and some cakes; coloured for decorating.*

Light and dark muscovado sugars: *Raw cane sugars add moisture, colour and a caramel flavour to cakes.*

Demerara sugar: *Unrefined with a low molasses content, this gives a good flavour to fruit and spice cakes.*

Dairy Produce

Store dairy products in the refrigerator or a cold pantry. If not fresh, they will taint and spoil the baking. Butter keeps for 2–3 weeks; eggs keep for 1–2 weeks; milk, cream and soft cheeses keep for 2–3 days.

Double cream: *Contains a high percentage of fat, which enables it to be whipped firmly without curdling.*

Cream or curd cheese: *Full-fat cream cheese is richer and more creamy. Curd cheese is lower in fat, drier in texture and slightly acidic.*

Ricotta cheese: *A slightly grainy, low-fat soft cheese with a sweet taste.*

Eggs: *Give flavour, colour and lightness to a cake. Use size 2 eggs unless the recipe states otherwise. Always use at room temperature.*

Milk: *Good for moistening and loosening thick cake mixtures. Also gives a softer crust to choux pastry. Full-fat milk is most commonly used.*

Sunflower or groundnut oil: *For rich moisture in some fruit sponges and spiced cakes.*

Butter: *Use lightly salted butter for cakes unless otherwise stated. Use unsalted for fillings and icings.*

Enriching Ingredients

Nuts, dried fruit and spices were used extensively in the general cuisine of ancient times. Today they are important for enriching cakes and pastries. Buy in small amounts as spices soon lose their pungency and nuts become rancid and bitter after 3–4 months. Dried fruit also spoils with time. Store in airtight containers in a cool, dry place.

Nuts & Dried Fruit

Almonds: *Available whole, ground or flaked, these are sweet to taste.*

Pistachio nuts: *Their distinctive green kernels add colour and flavour. Blanch before use.*

Pine nuts: *The soft, oily textured seed of the stone pine has a strong flavour that is enhanced by baking.*

Hazelnuts: *Roast first to bring out their rich flavour.*

Walnuts: *Rich in oil and protein, with an unmistakable flavour.*

Pecan nuts: *A relative of the walnut that is native to the USA.*

Coconut: *Freshly grated, it gives moisture to a cake. Thinly pared shavings make a pretty decoration.*

Sultanas: *These are small, seedless golden raisins. Augment the flavour by plumping in brandy before using.*

Figs: *Provide excellent fruity flavour with a seedy crunch. Buy them whole, remove the stalks and then cut by hand. They can be plumped up overnight in cold water.*

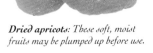

Dates: *A sun-dried fruit, these add moisture and sweet, rich flavour.*

Muscat raisins: *Dried Muscatel grapes; seedless ones are the best.*

Dried cranberries: *American red berries with a piquant flavour.*

Dried apricots: *These soft, moist fruits may be plumped up before use.*

Flavourings & Spices

Instant coffee powder: *An easy way to add rich coffee flavour.*

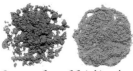

Cocoa powder and drinking chocolate powder: *Crushed from the "chocolate liquor" of dried, roasted cocoa beans.*

Dark rum: *A strongly aromatic and richly flavoured spirit distilled from sugar cane.*

Brandy: *Distilled from grapes, this spirit has a deep, mellow flavour.*

Kirsch: *A fiery, Eau de Vie made from crushed fermented cherries.*

Vanilla extract: *Made by macerating crushed vanilla pods in alcohol.*

Orange-flower water: *Strongly perfumed distilled flower essence.*

Tiny seeds lie inside the pod

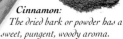

Nutmeg: *This dried kernel imparts a warm, richly aromatic flavour to many spiced cakes. Best used freshly grated.*

Vanilla pod and seeds: *Add a sweet, mellow flavour. Make vanilla sugar by placing a pod in a jar of caster sugar.*

Whole nutmeg

Allspice: *Also known as Jamaican pepper, this is sweet yet peppery.*

Poppy seeds: *Oily ripened seeds with a rich, nutty flavour.*

Cinnamon: *The dried bark or powder has a sweet, pungent, woody aroma.*

Cloves: *Dried flower buds with a bitter, sharp flavour, these can be bought whole or in powder form.*

Lemon and orange zest: *Contain the essential flavouring oils.*

Aniseed: *Adds a distinctive, sweet, liquorice-like flavour and can be bought as seed or a fine powder.*

Buy pieces with smooth skin

Fresh root ginger: *Gives a sharp, hot, aromatic flavour.*

Dried ground ginger: *A highly concentrated, spicy and hot flavour, so take care to use the correct measure.*

Saffron: *One of the most expensive spices, prized for its colour and taste.*

Decorating Ingredients

Even the simplest decorations enhance the texture and flavour of a cake. Fresh and glacé fruits have the greatest visual appeal with their tempting, bright and colourful appearance. Chocolate and coffee finishes give a wonderful rich look to cakes, and subtly coloured and finely flavoured icings offer luxurious stylishness with little effort.

Fresh Fruit

Raspberries: *Sweet, juicy ruby red berries; the richer their colour, the riper and more delicious they are.*

Grapes: *Select seedless varieties to embellish dessert-style cakes.*

Apples: *Choose crisp, shiny fruit with a good colour. Well-flavoured dessert apples are best for tarts and cakes as they stay whole during baking.*

Blueberries: *Deep purple-skinned berries with dark green flesh, these are sweet yet tart and acidic, and blend well with other soft fruit.*

Strawberries: *These have a sweet, refreshing flavour. Choose firm, undamaged fruit with an even colour and bright green tops.*

Oranges and lemons: *Strongly aromatic citrus fruit with a sweet acidic flavour. They add colour and help to neutralize any cloying sugariness in baking.*

Glacé Fruit

Glacé citron peel and clementines: *Buy good quality fruit that are soft-textured and not too sweet. Rinse off the excess sugar or syrup before using if wished.*

Mixed chopped peel: *Ready-cut orange and lemon peel is unsugared.*

Angelica: *The crystallized stem of a large garden herb.*

Natural and red glacé cherries: *Wash in warm water before baking to remove the sugary surface, then dry thoroughly on kitchen paper.*

Glacé pineapple: *Cut the whole circular slices to the size you require.*

Crystallized ginger: *Has a strong, sharp tang, so use sparingly.*

Preserves

Chestnut purée: The canned, unsweetened purée is good for using in cake fillings.

Seedless raspberry jam: Ideal as a sweet, distinctive filling in light sponge cakes.

Redcurrant jelly: Sharp, tangy and very fruity.

Apricot jam: Adds a sharp, fruity flavour and helps bond icing to a cake's surface.

Marmalade: Use this citrus fruit preserve as a glaze for a glacé fruit decoration.

Cranberry jelly: Crystal clear with a tart sweetness.

Chocolate

Chocolate buttons: Small chocolate discs are ideal for children's cakes.

Chocolate coffee beans: Roasted coffee beans covered in chocolate.

Chocolate shapes make easy decorations

Chocolate: Plain chocolate containing 50-70% cocoa solids has the richest and best flavour for baking. Milk and white chocolate have less flavour but are good for decoration.

Chocolate thins: Slim squares of chocolate can be made by hand or bought from quality confectioners. They make good decorations for cakes, whole, halved or cut into triangles.

Chocolate sticks: Narrow strips of flavoured milk or plain chocolate are useful for decorating both children's party cakes and more sophisticated chocolate cakes.

Colourings

Take care when using any food colourings as they are all very concentrated. Dip the tip of a fine skewer into the colouring, adding very gradually until the right shade is achieved. Remember that colours darken with time.

Red paste

Green liquid

Yellow liquid

Essential Tools & Baking Equipment

Here is a basic selection of the most useful equipment to have in the kitchen when you are baking cakes. A few more unusual items are also shown as they do make certain tasks much easier. When buying tools, always choose the best quality available: they last longer, are more reliable and achieve the best results. For successful baking, a set of accurate kitchen scales is also essential as ingredients must be measured carefully.

Palette knife: *Available in different sizes, with a long, wide flexible blade. Use for spreading and smoothing fillings and icings.*

Choose a palette knife with a flexible blade

Spoons: *Wooden spoons should have long handles and rounded bases. They are ideal for beating. Use a large metal spoon for folding in whisked egg whites.*

Spatula: *Long-handled, with a flexible rubber or plastic end for scraping mixture from the sides of a bowl.*

Long serrated knife: *Necessary for cutting cakes into thin layers.*

Balloon whisk: *When whisking egg whites and cream, this tool lends more control than an electric whisk.*

Biscuit cutters: *Varying sizes and shapes of plastic or metal cutters are needed for tartlet cases and biscuits.*

Rolling pin: *Must be completely smooth, at least 50cm (20in) long and have straight, unshaped ends. Essential for rolling out pastry and sugarpaste.*

Cake boards: *Lightweight boards covered in silver or gold paper are available in assorted sizes, shapes and thicknesses for the assembly of celebration cakes.*

Glass mixing bowls: The best bowls are made of strong, heatproof glass, and have smooth, rounded bases.

Grater: This should have one coarse and one fine grating face, and one coarse and one fine zesting face. Good for chocolate, fine citrus zest and fresh nutmeg.

Measuring jug: A clear, heatproof jug, showing both metric and imperial measurements is best.

Sieve: Use metal sieves for dry ingredients and plastic for fruit purées.

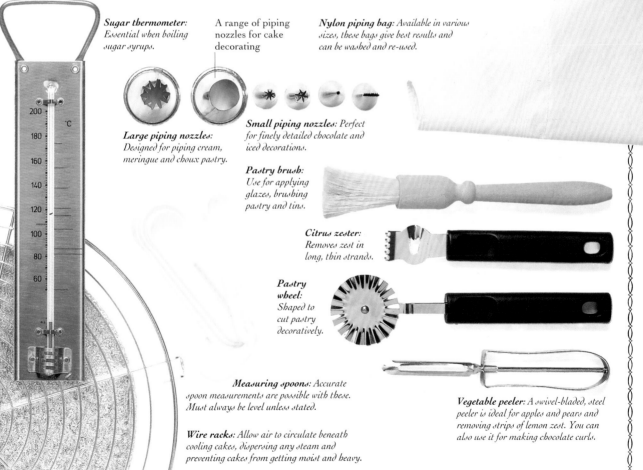

Sugar thermometer: Essential when boiling sugar syrups.

A range of piping nozzles for cake decorating

Nylon piping bag: Available in various sizes, these bags give best results and can be washed and re-used.

Large piping nozzles: Designed for piping cream, meringue and choux pastry.

Small piping nozzles: Perfect for finely detailed chocolate and iced decorations.

Pastry brush: Use for applying glazes, brushing pastry and tins.

Citrus zester: Removes zest in long, thin strands.

Pastry wheel: Shaped to cut pastry decoratively.

Measuring spoons: Accurate spoon measurements are possible with these. Must always be level unless stated.

Wire racks: Allow air to circulate beneath cooling cakes, dispersing any steam and preventing cakes from getting moist and heavy.

Vegetable peeler: A swivel-bladed, steel peeler is ideal for apples and pears and removing strips of lemon zest. You can also use it for making chocolate curls.

Bakeware

Choose good quality, heavyweight baking tins that conduct the heat efficiently and evenly. Matt-coloured metal tins or good quality non-stick tins are best. Inexpensive tins made from thin, lightweight metal soon buckle, wear out quickly and conduct heat badly, causing cakes to burn and cook unevenly. Also avoid cheap, shiny tins and glass bakeware. Wash, rinse and dry all bakeware thoroughly in a warm oven before and after use.

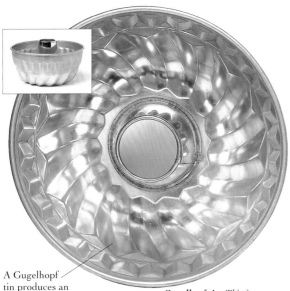

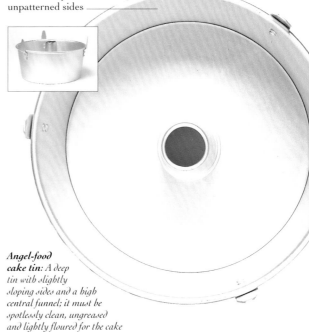

An Angel-food cake tin has plain, unpatterned sides

A Gugelhopf tin produces an attractive, shaped cake

Gugelhopf tin: *This deep, elaborately patterned, sloping-sided tin has a central funnel that helps the cake to bake through evenly and quickly.*

Angel-food cake tin: *A deep tin with slightly sloping sides and a high central funnel; it must be spotlessly clean, ungreased and lightly floured for the cake mixture to rise perfectly.*

Deep, round tin: *Loose- or fixed-base deep-sided tins available in various sizes are good for rich, heavily fruited cakes that require longer baking. Line with paper before using.*

Deep patty tin: *Use this type of tin for making small cheesecakes. Choose one with a non-stick finish.*

Swiss roll tin:
Ideal for roulades.

Flat baking sheet:
*Use for biscuits,
meringues and
choux pastry.*

**Victoria
Sandwich tins:**
*Shallow, straight-sided
tins with fixed or loose bases. Good
for baking sponge cake layers.*

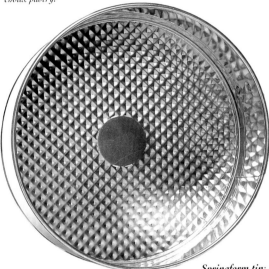

Flan tin: *This is
loose-based with fluted
sides and available in
different shapes, sizes and
depths. Choose one with deeper
sides if there is lots of filling.*

Springform tin: *A
loose-based tin with its
sides held together by a
spring-clip, making it
easier to remove the cake.*

Loaf tin: *A deep, rectangular tin
with rounded corners is perfect for
making tea breads. Tins are
available in 500g (1lb) and 1kg
(2lb) sizes. Line before using.*

A Balmoral tin
has decorative
ribbed sides

Deep, square tin: *With a loose or fixed
base, this is a tin for cakes that require
longer baking. Shallower tins are better
for sponge cakes and tray bakes.*

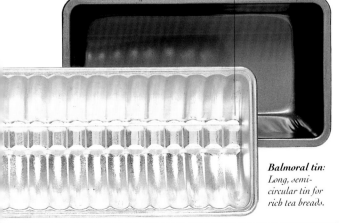

Balmoral tin:
*Long, semi-
circular tin for
rich tea breads.*

Preparing Cake Tins

The type and size of tin is crucial to a cake's success. Always use the size stated in the recipe and check by measuring across the top, from one inside wall to the other. Depth is also important: too shallow and the mixture will overflow; too deep and the cake will not rise properly. All tins require some form of preparation, depending on the style of cake.

Greasing & Lining

Preparing a cake tin helps to stop the cake from sticking, making it easier to remove. Odd-shaped tins should be greased twice with butter, then dusted with flour. Other tins can be lined with silicone paper, which has a non-stick finish, or greaseproof paper, which needs to be brushed with more butter. Rich fruit cakes also benefit from a paper collar around the tin to prevent them from over-browning and drying out.

HANDY TIPS
• *Make sure that all your bakeware is spotlessly clean and dry before you start.*
• *Greasing before lining keeps the paper in place.*

LINING A ROUND OR LARGE SQUARE TIN

1 Brush the inside of the tin evenly with melted butter. Cut one strip of paper to fit around the sides, overlapping slightly, making sure it is 5cm (2in) wider than the depth of the tin.

2 Fold in one long edge of the paper by 2.5cm (1in) and crease well. Unfold and then make angled cuts at 2.5cm (1in) intervals along this edge, up to the folded line.

Press the cut edge down on to the base of the tin

3 Drop the paper strip cut-side down into the tin so that the creased edge rests in the join at the base of the tin. Press the paper well on to the buttered sides and base of the cake tin.

4 Place the base of the tin on another piece of paper. Draw a faint pencil line neatly around the base. Cut out the paper circle just inside the pencil line so that the paper disc will fit snugly into the bottom of the cake tin.

5 Smooth the paper circle on to the base of the tin, making sure that the cut edge lies flat underneath it. If using greaseproof paper, brush once more with melted butter.

Place the paper in the base of the tin

MAKING A BROWN PAPER COLLAR

Line the cake tin as before with paper. Fold a few sheets of brown paper or newspaper into a long strip to match the depth and diameter of the cake tin. Wrap around the outside of the tin and secure in place with string. Rest the tin on a baking sheet protected with another few sheets of folded paper.

LINING A SMALL SQUARE OR LOAF TIN

DUSTING WITH FLOUR

1 Place the tin in the middle of a sheet of paper, large enough to extend up the sides and beyond by 2.5cm (1in). Draw around the base. Crease along these lines. From the longer sides, cut along the creases up to the marked lines.

2 Grease the base and sides of the tin. Fold up the sides of the rectangle and drop into the tin, tucking the flaps behind the longer sides. Press on to the base and sides, securing the paper in place at the corners with more butter.

Grease the base and sides of the tin and leave to set in the refrigerator for a few minutes. Repeat once more. Spoon in a little flour and tilt the tin until the sides are evenly coated. Turn over and tap the base to remove any excess.

General Baking Skills

Once baking begins it is essential to avoid any interruption so that the steps of preparation may follow each other in quick succession. All the ingredients should be ready prepared – weighed, sifted, ground, melted or grated – before you start to combine them. Cake tins should also be greased and lined and the oven preheated to the correct temperature.

SIFTING FLOUR

Shake the flour twice through a fine sieve held high over a bowl. This fills it with air and improves the cake's texture. Sift once more with any additional dry ingredients so they are evenly mixed.

SEPARATING EGGS

Carefully crack the shell on the edge of a clean bowl. Break the egg open and without splitting the yolk, quickly pour it from one half shell to the other, letting the white fall into the bowl below.

ZESTING CITRUS FRUIT

Rub the skin of a scrubbed or unwaxed lemon over the finest side of a grater, without removing any of the bitter white pith underneath. A citrus zester (see page 39) removes longer strands.

MELTING CHOCOLATE

Melt the chocolate until smooth and glossy

Break the chocolate into pieces and place in a small heatproof bowl. Rest over a saucepan of barely simmering water and leave for about 5 minutes, stirring now and then, until melted.

ROASTING HAZELNUTS

1 Roast on a baking sheet at 180°C/ 350°F/gas 4 for 15 minutes, until lightly browned and with flaking skins.

2 Tip the hot nuts on to a cloth. Fold the cloth over them and rub gently to remove the skins. Cool before using.

WHIPPING CREAM

Pour the cream into a bowl and whip with a balloon whisk or an electric mixer until it has formed soft peaks that turn over at the ends. For piping, whip the cream until it forms slightly stiffer peaks, but be careful not to over-whip, especially in warm conditions, or the cream will curdle and separate. Chantilly cream is whipped cream sweetened with sugar and flavoured with brandy or vanilla. It can be used as a filling or decoration.

HANDY TIPS

◆ *Always use cream straight from the refrigerator or it may separate.*

◆ *Only use double cream for decoration; whipping cream will not hold its shape.*

BLANCHING PISTACHIOS

Drop shelled pistachios into boiling water and leave for 2–3 minutes. Drain, slide off the skins and leave to dry before using.

TOASTING BREADCRUMBS

Spread slices of stale crustless bread on a wire rack. Bake at 140°C/275°F/ gas 1 for 45 minutes–1 hour until dry, crisp and golden. Cool and break into pieces. Either grind to a powder in a food processor or place in a plastic bag and crush with a rolling pin. Sift through a fine-meshed sieve to remove the coarser crumbs.

Soft peaks with the cream turning over at the end

DISSOLVING GELATINE

Gelatine needs to be softened, or "sponged", in cold liquid and then dissolved before using. Cool the dissolved gelatine before blending into a mixture or it will form strings. Use 1 teaspoon of gelatine powder to 1 tablespoon of liquid.

HANDY TIPS

◆ *Always add the gelatine to the liquid or lumps will form and it will not dissolve properly.*

◆ *Do not over-heat the gelatine or it will lose its setting abilities.*

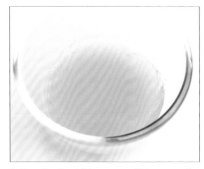

1 Put the liquid into a small heatproof bowl. Sprinkle over the gelatine and leave to "sponge" for 5 minutes.

2 Sit the bowl in a small pan of barely simmering water. Leave until clear and dissolved. Cool before using.

Basic Methods

Creaming and whisking are the two main methods for making cakes. The ingredients must always be handled with care and should be at room temperature before you start.

Incorporate as much air as possible while beating or whisking: an electric mixer will make this a lot easier. Then lightly fold in the additional ingredients by hand.

CREAMED CAKE MIXTURES

These cakes have a moist, slightly close texture. Vigorous "creaming" together of the butter, sugar and eggs incorporates the air that is essential to produce a good cake.

The mixture should be smooth and fluffy before you add the eggs

1 Beat the butter in a mixing bowl for 1–2 minutes until soft and creamy. Add the sugar and beat vigorously for 3–5 minutes until it is pale and fluffy and doubled in volume (right).

2 Beat in the eggs, one at a time (left), beating well between each addition. The mixture will initially slacken, then thicken when ready for the next egg.

3 Spoon the already sifted flour into the sieve. Hold the sieve a little way above the bowl and sift once more over the creamed mixture.

5 The finished cake mixture should be smooth, thick and creamy and drop reluctantly off the spoon.

4 Gently fold in the flour with a large metal spoon, using a cutting and folding action. Do not stir or beat the mixture or the added air will be lost.

WHISKING EGG WHITES

If whisking egg whites to fold into a cake mixture, do not whisk them too stiffly: they will not blend in evenly, making the cake look patchy.

Whisked egg whites with soft peaks

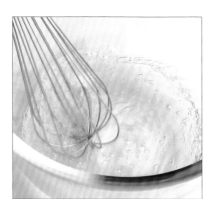

1 Place the egg whites in a spotlessly clean bowl. Using a balloon whisk or an electric mixer, whisk the egg whites slowly, until foamy.

2 Start to beat the egg whites faster, until they form a snow which stands in peaks that are still soft enough for the ends to turn over.

WHISKED CAKE MIXTURES

Whisked cakes have a very light, delicate, open texture. Bake them immediately: if left to stand the mixture will collapse.

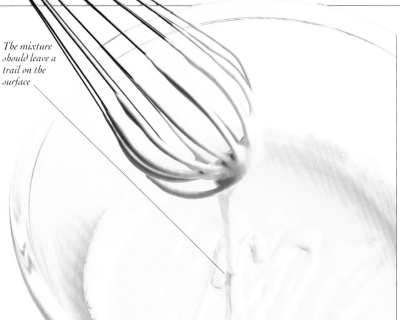

The mixture should leave a trail on the surface

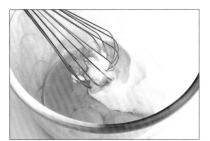

1 Whisk the egg yolks and sugar in a large bowl to the "ribbon stage"; the mixture will be pale, thick and doubled in volume. If drizzled over the surface it holds its shape for 4–5 seconds (right).

2 Whisk the egg whites into soft peaks. Stir 2 large spoonfuls into the egg yolk mixture to loosen the texture slightly. Sift over and gently fold in the flour using a large metal spoon.

3 Trickle the melted butter around the edge of the mixture, without adding the milky sediment, and gently fold it in.

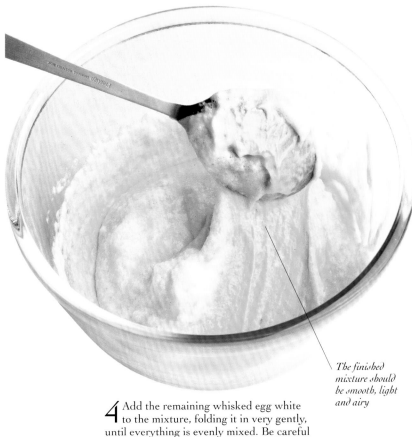

The finished mixture should be smooth, light and airy

4 Add the remaining whisked egg white to the mixture, folding it in very gently, until everything is evenly mixed. Be careful not to overwork the mixture.

MAKING SIMPLE MERINGUES

The whisking of egg whites traps air; adding cream of tartar and sugar helps to stabilize the mixture and prevents it from separating.

1 Whisk the egg whites until foamy. Add the cream of tartar and whisk into soft peaks. Gradually whisk in half the sugar, 1 tablespoon at a time.

2 Either fold in the rest of the sugar a few spoonfuls at a time, using a large metal spoon, or to form a stiffer meringue for piping, continue to whisk it in gradually.

Whisk the meringue until dense and stiff peaks form

SHAPING MERINGUES

For individual meringues, push large spoonfuls of mixture on to silicone paper-lined baking sheets.

MAKING MERINGUE DISCS

1 Spoon the meringue mixture into a nylon piping bag fitted with a 1cm (½in) plain nozzle.

2 Mark circles on a lined baking sheet. Pipe from the centre outwards, in a continuous spiral, to just inside the line.

Pipe just within the marked circle

3 To check that a meringue is done, lift it off the paper, turn it over and gently tap the underside. It should sound hollow and be crisp and dry to the touch.

Cooking & Turning Out Cakes

Cakes generally cook best in the centre of a preheated oven. Check that the racks are in position and that the temperature is correct before placing the cake inside. Avoid opening the door once the cake has started to bake until at least three-quarters of the cooking time has passed because a sudden draught will cause the unstable structure to collapse.

CHECKING FOR READINESS

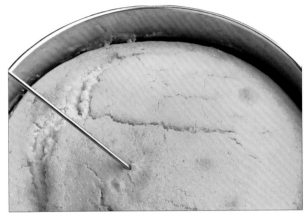

A cooked sponge cake should be well risen, golden and just starting to shrink away from the sides of the tin. It should also spring back when you press the top softly with a finger.

All types of cakes may be tested by inserting a fine metal skewer into the centre. The skewer should come out clean. If any mixture clings to it, bake for another 5 minutes.

TURNING OUT

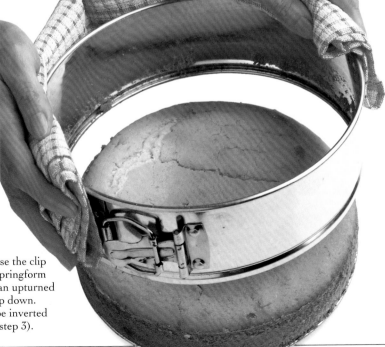

1 Leave the cake to rest in the tin for a few minutes. If unlined, run a round-bladed knife around the inside edge of the tin to loosen the sides of the cake.

2 To take out of the tin, release the clip and remove the sides of a springform tin. Stand loose-based tins on an upturned basin and allow the sides to slip down. Cakes in solid-based tins can be inverted straight on to a wire rack (see step 3).

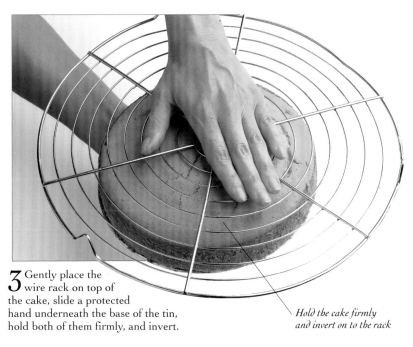

4 Slide a palette knife between the cake and the tin base and remove. Carefully peel off the lining paper without tearing the delicate structure of the cake, and leave to cool.

HANDY TIPS

◆ *If more than one cake is being baked at a time, they may need rotating in the oven and may take a little longer to cook.*

◆ *For a layered cake that needs a smooth, flat top, cool the cake with the base-side uppermost.*

3 Gently place the wire rack on top of the cake, slide a protected hand underneath the base of the tin, hold both of them firmly, and invert.

Hold the cake firmly and invert on to the rack

TURNING OUT A ROULADE

For undecorated roulades, remove the sponge from the oven and turn out on to greaseproof or silicone paper sprinkled with caster sugar.

Turn out using an oven cloth

2 Pull out the edges of the paper from underneath the roulade. Release the paper at one corner and slowly peel back, taking care not to tear the delicate sponge, especially at the edges. The cake is now ready to be filled and rolled.

1 Quickly invert the hot roulade on to the prepared paper and carefully lift off the tin.

HANDY TIPS

◆ *Turning the roulade out on to sugar stops it from sticking to the paper.*

◆ *Roulades that are turned out while hot must be rolled up immediately or they will crack.*

Layering, Rolling & Storing Cakes

The plainest cakes taste exquisitely rich when layered up with special fillings. Some of the more elaborately layered cakes do take a little effort to complete so allow plenty of time for assembling them and then chill for at least 4–5 hours to allow the layers to settle and the flavours to blend. Correctly storing cakes will enable you to eat them at their best.

LAYERING

1 Place the cake on a firm, level surface. Rest a hand lightly on top of the cake to hold it steady. Slice the cake horizontally through the centre with a sharp, long-bladed, serrated knife.

2 Starting with the top layer, carefully separate the cake layers by sliding the thin base of a flan tin between them. When each layer is fully supported, lift off and set to one side until needed.

3 For additional flavour, lightly sprinkle each cake layer with a little liqueur or flavoured sugar syrup (see page 153). Leave to soak in well before layering up with the filling.

4 Starting with the bottom cake layer, spread each one evenly with a portion of the filling, to within 5mm (¼in) of the edge. Cover with the next layer and press down gently.

Spread the filling in an even layer

5 Neatly even up the edges of the buttercream layers before finishing.

HANDY TIP

♦ *Simple sponge cakes are best filled and eaten on the day they are made. Some of the more lavishly filled cakes taste better if they are left to mature for a day or two before serving.*

FILLING A ROULADE

1 Using a large palette knife, carefully spread the filling in an even layer over the surface of the warm, turned-out roulade, taking it to within 1cm (½in) of the edge.

2 Neatly trim about 1cm (½in) off each of the edges. Using the back of a large knife, score a shallow, straight line along one short end of the sponge, about 2.5cm (1in) in from the edge.

3 With the scored end facing you, lift up the edge of the paper and use it to help support and guide the cake as you roll it up. Gently roll the roulade over so that the seam lies underneath.

4 Cut about 1cm (½in) off each end of the roulade to give a neat finish. Leave to cool on a wire rack. Carefully lift up the roulade using two large palette knives and transfer to a serving plate, seam-side down.

A roulade looks attractive with a contrasting filling

--- *HANDY TIP* ---

♦ *Roulades that are to be filled with fresh cream or buttercream need to be covered with silicone paper, then a slightly damp tea towel and left to cool before turning out, filling and rolling. This prevents them from drying out.*

CUTTING CAKES

Cutting the first slice of a cake is always difficult. Using a long, sharp, pointed knife, lightly insert the tip into the centre of the cake. Holding it at right angles to the cake, gently cut downwards through the layers with a slight sawing action. Determine the size of the slice, then make a second cut in the same way. Slide the blade of the knife as far under the slice as you can and gently start to ease it out. If it won't come away easily, then carefully re-cut either side of the slice. Subsequent slices will be easier!

SERVING CAKES

As time and trouble have been taken to prepare a cake, a little effort in its presentation is worthwhile. Choose a serving plate that matches the cake's character – for example, elegant, delicate china for an elaborate, multi-layered extravaganza or a plain, country-style plate for a more simple cake. Present the slice with some ceremony on a matching small tea-plate, with a cake fork on the side and a napkin at hand if you wish. The added effort and attention to such detail will be appreciated.

STORING & FREEZING

Cakes must be well wrapped to prevent them from drying out. A layered cake filled with cream or chocolate is best kept refrigerated in a large, airtight plastic box; one with a flat base and domed lid is ideal. Other layered cakes must be stored in a cool place. Wrap undecorated cakes in greaseproof paper then foil and store in an airtight container. To freeze, wrap the cake in greaseproof paper or foil and place in a freezer bag. Remove the air, then seal, label and date. Defrost, still wrapped, in a cool place or in the refrigerator.

Pastry Making

Pâte brisée, or shortcrust pastry, is very slightly sweetened with a small amount of sugar. *Pâte sucrée*, or sweet shortcrust pastry, is a sweeter, shorter pastry. It can either be pressed into the tin or rolled out between sheets of silicone paper. *Pâte sablée*, or sweet flan pastry, is very short and crisp, and ideal for all sweet flans.

One quantity of each recipe below will line a 24cm (9½ in) flan tin.

PATE BRISEE

INGREDIENTS

180g (6oz) plain flour, sifted
pinch of salt
100g (3½oz) chilled butter
2 tbsp caster sugar
1 egg yolk, lightly beaten
1–2 tbsp iced water

1 Sift the flour once more, together with the salt, into a large mixing bowl or on to a clean work surface. Make a well in the centre.

2 Cut the chilled butter into pieces and add to the flour. Lightly rub the butter and the flour together with the tips of your fingers, lifting the mixture and letting it fall back down, until you have a fine, crumb-like mixture.

Lightly fork the sugar through the mixture

3 Add the caster sugar to the bowl and stir in with a fork, making sure it is evenly distributed throughout the mixture.

4 Mix the egg yolk with the water until well blended. Drizzle over the mixture while stirring continuously with a small, round-bladed knife.

6 Gently bring the small lumps of pastry together using the heel of the hand until they form a rough ball. The quicker you do this the better.

5 Working swiftly yet lightly, continue to stir everything together until the mixture starts to stick together in little lumps.

——— HANDY TIPS ———
♦ *Pastry will keep in the refrigerator for 4–5 days, tightly wrapped in clingfilm.*
♦ *Chilling the pastry before rolling out prevents it from shrinking during baking.*

The dough should form a neat ball

7 Knead briefly on a lightly floured work surface until smooth. Wrap in clingfilm and chill for at least 1 hour.

VARIATION WITH PROCESSOR

Sift the flour, salt and sugar into the bowl of the food processor. Add the chilled butter pieces and blend in short bursts for approximately 10–15 seconds or until it has formed a fine, crumb-like mixture. Do not allow the crumbs to form into large lumps as this will over-work the mixture. Mix the egg yolk with a teaspoon of water (less water is needed for this method). With the motor running, quickly pour the liquid into the bowl and blend for a few seconds until the mixture has formed a well-compacted ball. Turn the pastry out on to a lightly floured surface, knead briefly and gently until smooth, then wrap tightly in clingfilm and chill for at least 1 hour before using.

PATE SUCREE

INGREDIENTS

170g (5¾ oz) plain flour
pinch of salt
100g (3½ oz) chilled butter
60g (2oz) caster sugar
1 tsp finely grated lemon zest
1 egg yolk, lightly beaten
1–2 tbsp iced water

Make the pastry following the main recipe for Pâte Brisée, adding the grated lemon zest with the sugar. Chill well before using – overnight if possible or for at least 1 hour. Allow the pastry to come back to room temperature, then knead briefly before using.

PATE SABLEE

INGREDIENTS

180g (6oz) plain flour, sifted
90g (3oz) chilled butter
60g (2oz) icing sugar, sifted
1 tsp finely grated lemon zest
1 egg yolk, lightly beaten
1–2 tbsp iced water

Make the pastry following the main recipe for Pâte Brisée, adding the grated lemon zest with the icing sugar. Chill the pastry well before using – overnight if possible or for at least 1 hour. Allow the pastry to come back to room temperature, then knead briefly before using.

MAKING A PASTRY CASE

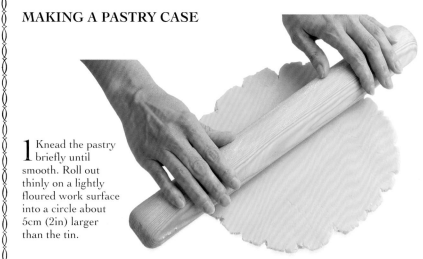

1 Knead the pastry briefly until smooth. Roll out thinly on a lightly floured work surface into a circle about 5cm (2in) larger than the tin.

2 Lightly rest the rolling pin over the centre of the pastry. Fold one side of the pastry over the pin, carefully lift the pastry across the tin and unroll.

3 Using floured fingers, carefully ease the pastry into the bottom and up the sides of the tin. Make sure that the pastry is well pressed into the join where the base and sides meet.

4 Ease the excess pastry out over the edge of the flan tin. Run a rolling pin over the top of the tin to remove it. Patch any breaks in the pastry with the trimmings, sealing with a little water.

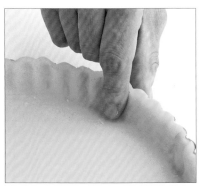

5 Firmly press the pastry on to the sides of the flan tin, whether fluted or plain, using your index finger. Chill for at least 1 hour to help prevent shrinkage during baking.

6 To "bake blind", prick the base of the pastry case all over with a fork. Line neatly with a single sheet of greaseproof paper or a double thickness of aluminium foil.

7 Fill the paper-lined case with a thin layer of dried pulses, rice or ceramic pastry beans. This will prevent the base from rising and keep the sides in place. Bake according to the recipe.

Pastry case ready to bake blind

HANDY TIPS

♦ *Make sure the pastry is at room temperature before rolling it out.*

♦ *If the baked case is to contain a moist filling, brush the hot pastry with egg white to seal.*

CHOUX PASTRY

Choux pastry gets its name from the French phrase *pâte à chaud*, meaning heated pastry, as it is cooked twice. The paste puffs up to three times its size when done.

INGREDIENTS

125g (4oz) strong plain flour
pinch of salt
2 tsp caster sugar
100g (3½ oz) butter
250ml (8fl oz) water
4 eggs, lightly beaten

1 Sift the flour, salt and sugar on to creased greaseproof paper. Melt the butter in the water in a large, heavy-based pan. Bring to a fast, rolling boil.

2 Take off the heat, tip in the flour, return to the heat and beat rapidly into a smooth, glossy paste that rolls cleanly off the sides and base of the pan.

3 Allow the paste to cool for about 5 minutes. Then start to beat in the egg, a little at a time.

4 Continue adding the egg until the mixture is smooth and glossy – you will probably only need about 3½ eggs. Reserve the rest for glazing. Spoon into a piping bag fitted with a plain nozzle.

The mixture should fall reluctantly from the spoon

5 Pipe small mounds of paste on to the prepared baking sheet. Glaze with the rest of the egg. Bake for 15–20 minutes. Pierce the bases with a skewer and bake a further 5 minutes. Cool on a wire rack.

HANDY TIPS

- *Run a lightly greased baking sheet under cold water and leave slightly wet.*
- *Pipe the puffs well apart on to the baking sheet.*

3

Recipes

A classic collection of recipes dating
back to the 16th century is provided
in this international repertoire of
cakes, ranging from the Kastella of
Japan, to Hungarian Poppy Seed
and Chocolate Torte, and an
American Pecan and Maple Pie. The
selection includes traditional cakes
for festivals and weddings, as well as
exciting ideas for children's birthday
cakes. There is something
here to please everyone.

Butter Cakes

Simple butter cakes are very easy to make. They are based on a combination of the key cake ingredients: butter, sugar, eggs and flour, in varying proportions. These recipes are for plain, wholesome cakes that are satisfyingly rich with a buttery texture and excellent flavour, ideal for serving with a cup of coffee or at afternoon tea. Although they are not elaborate, the addition of special ingredients such as chocolate, fresh fruit, spices or nuts, together with a coating of sweet glacé icing, readily transforms them into memorable treats.

Pound Cake

In her book of 1747, The Art of Cookery made Plain and Easy, *Hannah Glasse explained how to "Make a Pound Cake" using a pound of flour, a pound of butter, a pound of sugar, eight eggs and "a great wooden Spoon". Today we no longer have to make such large quantities or rely on the spoon – using a machine makes much lighter work.*

INGREDIENTS

125g (4oz) plain flour, sifted
125g (4oz) potato flour
1 tsp baking powder
250g (8oz) butter
250g (8oz) caster sugar
seeds from ¼ of a vanilla pod
4 large eggs (size 1)
1 tsp finely grated lemon zest
1 tbsp milk
icing sugar to decorate

1 Sift the plain flour, potato flour and baking powder together. Set aside. Beat the butter, caster sugar and vanilla seeds together until pale and fluffy. Beat in the eggs, one at a time, adding a little of the flour if the mixture begins to curdle. Beat in the lemon zest.

2 Gradually beat in the flour until everything is evenly mixed. Stir in the milk. Spoon the mixture into the prepared tin and bake in the preheated oven for 1 hour or until a skewer inserted into the cake comes out clean.

3 Remove the cake from the oven, ease away from the sides of the tin and leave to rest for 10 minutes. Turn out on to a wire rack and leave to cool. Transfer to a serving plate and dust with a little icing sugar to decorate.

VARIATIONS

Fresh Fruit Pound Cake
Make the basic mixture, omitting the milk. Stone and roughly chop 250g (8oz) apricots, apples, plums or peaches into 1cm (½in) pieces. Stir in 1 tablespoon lemon juice and fold the fruit into the basic mixture. Bake for 1¼ hours. Decorate with 1 quantity lemon glacé icing (see page 152) and fine lemon shreds (see page 149) once the cake is cold.

Chocolate Marble Pound Cake
Make the basic mixture, omitting the milk. Put half into another bowl and stir in 2 tablespoons cocoa powder blended with 2 tablespoons dark rum and 75g (2½oz) melted plain chocolate (see page 44). Drop alternating spoonfuls of each mixture into the prepared tin and bake for 1 hour. Decorate with 1 quantity chocolate glacé icing (see page 152) once the cake is cold.

Mixed Spice Pound Cake
Sift 1 teaspoon ground cinnamon and ½ teaspoon grated nutmeg with the flour. Fold into the basic mixture with 60g (2oz) chopped roasted hazelnuts (see page 45). Bake for 1 hour. Decorate with caster sugar, cinnamon and chopped hazelnuts once cold.

 Oven temperature
180°C/350°F/gas 4

 Baking time
1 hour; 1¼ hours for the fresh fruit cakes

 Cake tin
1.5 litre (2½ pint) Gugelhopf mould, greased twice with melted butter and floured

 Makes
12–16 slices

 Storage
Fruit cakes keep for 2–3 days; others for 5–6 days

BASIC POUND CAKE *liberally dusted with vanilla-flavoured or plain caster sugar.*

CHOCOLATE MARBLE POUND CAKE *topped with a chocolate glacé icing.*

MIXED SPICE POUND CAKE *decorated with cinnamon, sugar and hazelnuts.*

FRESH APRICOT POUND CAKE *crowned with glacé icing and lemon shreds.*

Swedish Butter Ring

This treat may be eaten as it is or spread with butter. It should be eaten the day it is made, or better still while it is slightly warm from the oven.

INGREDIENTS

For the filling

90g (3oz) glacé cherries, chopped
90g (3oz) candied orange and lemon peel, finely chopped
1 tsp finely grated orange zest
3 tbsp fine shred marmalade

For the pastry

250g (8oz) self-raising flour
125g (4oz) butter, cut into small pieces
60g (2oz) semolina
60g (2oz) caster sugar
1 egg
2 tbsp milk

For the decoration

1 tbsp milk for brushing
1 tbsp preserving sugar crystals

1 For the filling, mix together the cherries, candied peel and orange zest. Set aside.

2 For the pastry, sift the flour into a bowl, add the butter and rub together into a fine crumb-like mixture. Stir in the semolina and sugar. Mix the egg with the milk. Stir into the dry mixture until everything begins to stick together and then knead briefly until smooth.

3 Roll out the pastry on a lightly floured surface into a 30x24cm (12x9½in) rectangle. Spread over the marmalade to within 5cm (2in) of each long edge. Sprinkle over the filling.

4 Starting with one long edge, roll up the pastry and then twist it into a ring, pinching the edges together at the join to seal. Carefully lift on to the prepared baking sheet and pinch together any large cracks with your fingers. Put a greased 5cm (2in) round metal biscuit cutter into the centre of the ring.

5 For the decoration, brush the ring with the milk and sprinkle with the sugar. Bake in the preheated oven for 25–30 minutes or until golden. Remove from the oven, carefully transfer to a wire rack, and leave to cool slightly. Serve warm, spread lightly with butter if you wish.

 Oven temperature
200°C/400°F/gas 6

 Baking time
25–30 minutes

 Cake tin
Flat baking sheet, greased

 Makes
8 slices

 Storage
Best eaten the day it is made

Hungarian Coffee Cake with Soured Cream

Traditionally served with steaming hot cups of strong coffee, this delicious cake contains layers of cinnamon and chopped nuts.

INGREDIENTS

For the cake

180g (6oz) butter
125g (4oz) caster sugar
1 tbsp vanilla sugar
2 eggs
150ml (¼ pint) soured cream
275g (9oz) plain flour
2 tsp baking powder
½ tsp bicarbonate of soda
pinch of salt

For the filling

100g (3½ oz) caster sugar
2 tsp ground cinnamon
100g (3½ oz) pecan nuts or walnuts, chopped

1 For the cake, beat the butter, caster sugar and vanilla sugar together until pale and fluffy. Beat in the eggs, one at a time, followed by the soured cream.

2 Sift the flour, baking powder, bicarbonate of soda and salt together. Add to the butter mixture and beat together well.

3 For the filling, mix the sugar, cinnamon and nuts together with a fork. Spoon one third of the cake mixture into the prepared tin and sprinkle over one third of the filling. Repeat twice more, ending with filling.

4 Bake in the preheated oven for 50 minutes–1 hour. Remove from the oven and leave for 5 minutes. Turn out of the tin and cool on a wire rack.

 Oven temperature
180°C/350°F/gas 4

 Baking time
50 minutes–1 hour

 Cake tin
20cm (8in) deep, round tin, greased and floured

 Makes
12 slices

 Storage
Keeps for 2 days

 Freezing
Freezes for 1–2 months

Lemon Syrup Butter Cake

This is one of those cut-and-come-again cakes that no one can resist. It has a sharp, fruity tang and is quick and easy to make.

INGREDIENTS

For the cake

125g (4oz) butter

125g (4oz) caster sugar

1 tbsp finely grated lemon zest

1 tbsp finely grated orange zest

2 large eggs (size 1)

125g (4oz) plain flour, sifted

½ tsp baking powder

2 tbsp warm water

For the syrup

2 tbsp lemon juice

2 tbsp orange juice

100g (3½oz) granulated sugar

1 For the cake, beat the butter, caster sugar, lemon zest and orange zest together in a large bowl until pale and fluffy. Beat in the eggs, one at a time, adding a little of the flour with the second egg if the mixture begins to curdle.

2 Sift the remaining flour and baking powder together. Beat into the butter mixture, followed by the water.

3 Spoon the mixture into the prepared tin and bake in the preheated oven for 45 minutes or until a skewer inserted into the cake comes out clean.

4 For the syrup, put the lemon juice, orange juice and sugar into a small heavy-based pan and heat gently until the sugar has dissolved. Keep warm.

5 Remove the cake from the oven and prick the top here and there with a fine skewer. Spoon over half the syrup and leave for 2–3 minutes. Turn out on to a wire rack and peel off the lining paper. Prick the base of the cake, pour over the rest of the syrup and leave to cool.

 Oven temperature
180°C/350°F/gas 4

 Baking time
45 minutes

 Cake tin
500g (1lb) loaf tin, greased and base-lined

 Makes
12 slices

 Storage
Keeps for 1 week

 Freezing
Freezes for 1–2 months

Blitzkuchen

Similar to a pound cake mixture that is baked in a shallow tin, these buttery slices are topped with a delicious cinnamon-spiced almond crumble.

INGREDIENTS

For the cake

2 eggs

125g (4oz) caster sugar

125g (4oz) plain flour, sifted

125g (4oz) butter, melted and cooled

1 tsp finely grated lemon zest

For the topping

100g (3½oz) plain flour, sifted

2 tsp ground cinnamon

60g (2oz) granulated sugar

75g (2½oz) ground almonds

75g (2½oz) unsalted butter, melted and cooled

1 For the cake, beat the eggs and sugar together until pale and frothy. Beat in the flour, followed by the melted butter and lemon zest, until everything is evenly mixed. Pour the mixture into the prepared tin, making sure the corners are well filled.

2 For the topping, sift the flour and cinnamon together into another bowl. Stir in the granulated sugar and ground almonds. Gradually pour in the melted butter, mixing all the time with a fork, until you have a coarse, crumb-like mixture.

3 Sprinkle the crumb mixture evenly over the surface of the cake mixture. Bake in the preheated oven for about 25–30 minutes or until golden. Remove from the oven, cut into slices and leave to cool in the tin on a wire rack. Remove from the tin once cold.

VARIATION

For a different topping, mix 75g (2½oz) flaked almonds with 1 teaspoon ground cinnamon and 2 tablespoons granulated sugar. Sprinkle evenly over the surface of the cake mixture and bake as for the main recipe.

 Oven temperature
190°C/375°F/gas 5

 Baking time
25–30 minutes

 Cake tin
18x28x3.5cm (7x11x1½in) shallow, rectangular tin, greased and lined

 Makes
15 slices

Storage
Keeps for 3–4 days

Sponge Cakes

Sponge *biscuit* appeared in European cookery manuscripts as early as the mid-16th century, sometimes softly textured but often as a hard biscuit. The egg mixture was usually heated then tediously whipped to cool it down. Today, the cold method uses separated eggs and takes much less time. Whisked and creamed sponge cakes remain favourites in any cook's repertoire. Their light and airy structure gives a delicious background for soft fruit and whipped cream, for aromatic spices, nutty textures, and fruity spirits, and of course, for chocolate.

Whipped cream laced with Kirsch adds to the delicious contrast of flavours

Fresh strawberries and raspberries make a tempting decoration

Biscuit de Savoie

INGREDIENTS

For the cake

60g (2oz) plain flour
60g (2oz) potato flour
180g (6oz) icing sugar, sifted
5 eggs, separated
pinch of salt
2 tsp lemon juice
½ tsp orange-flower water or 1 tsp dark rum

For the filling and decoration

90ml (6 tbsp) Kirsch-flavoured syrup (see page 155)
250g (8oz) fresh strawberries
250g (8oz) fresh raspberries
4 tbsp caster sugar
450ml (¾ pint) double cream
1 tbsp Kirsch
strawberry leaves and icing sugar

In France, Germany and Austria, biscuit is the customary name for light sponge cakes. Potato flour and eggs are the key ingredients for producing this light, airy mixture. It is especially suitable for layered and rolled cakes that require a firmer and slightly drier sponge.

1 For the cake, sift the flour and potato flour together three times. Set aside.

2 Reserve 3 tablespoons of the icing sugar. Whisk the remaining icing sugar and the egg yolks together to the ribbon stage (see page 48).

3 In another bowl, whisk the egg whites and salt into soft peaks (see page 47). Sift over the reserved sugar and whisk until they form slightly stiffer peaks. Fold in the lemon juice.

4 Stir 2 large spoonfuls of the egg white into the egg yolk mixture to loosen the texture. Gently fold in the flour and the orange-flower water or rum. Carefully fold in the remaining egg whites, taking care not to knock out the air.

5 Pour the mixture into the prepared tin and bake in the centre of the preheated oven for 35–40 minutes or until a

skewer inserted into the centre of the cake comes out clean.

6 Remove from the oven and leave to rest in the tin for 5–10 minutes. Turn out on to a wire rack and leave to cool. Peel off the lining paper once cold.

TO FINISH THE CAKE

1 Slice the cake horizontally into three layers. Sprinkle the bottom two layers with the Kirsch-flavoured syrup. Place the bottom layer on a serving plate, syrup-side up.

2 Set aside a few of the best strawberries and raspberries for the decoration. Remove the stalks from the remaining strawberries and cut them into quarters. Mix the raspberries with 1 tablespoon of the caster sugar. Whip the cream, the remaining caster sugar and the Kirsch into stiff peaks.

3 Carefully spoon the quartered strawberries evenly over the bottom cake layer, to within 1cm (½in) of the edge. Spoon over one third of the whipped cream and spread evenly over the fruit. Cover with the second syrup-soaked cake layer, syrup-side up. Spoon over the raspberries and spread out, followed by another third of the cream. Cover with the top cake layer and press it down lightly so that the fruit becomes embedded in the cream.

4 For the decoration, spread the remaining cream evenly over the top of the cake, using a palette knife. Arrange the reserved whole strawberries and raspberries in the centre and decorate with strawberry leaves. Dust lightly with icing sugar just before serving.

  Oven temperature 180°C/350°F/gas 4

 Baking time 35–40 minutes

 Cake tin 22cm (8½in) springform tin, greased and base-lined

 Makes 8–10 slices

 Storage Keeps for 2–3 days in the refrigerator

 Freezing Freezes for 1 month, undecorated

Step ahead Make the Kirsch-flavoured syrup

BISCUIT DE SAVOIE *combines delicate sponge, Kirsch-flavoured cream and juicy summer berries.*

Victoria Sandwich

A traditional recipe in the British baking repertoire, and similar to Pound Cake (see page 60) in proportions. This simple, fool-proof recipe is quick and easy to make using the creamed method (see page 46).

INGREDIENTS

250g (8oz) butter, softened

250g (8oz) caster sugar

4 eggs

250g (8oz) self-raising flour

1–2 tbsp milk

4 tbsp seedless raspberry jam

caster sugar to decorate

1 In a large bowl, beat the butter and caster sugar together until pale and fluffy. Beat in the eggs, one at a time, beating in a little of the flour if the mixture begins to curdle.

2 Sift the remaining flour over the surface of the mixture and fold it in, followed by a little milk to give the mixture a soft dropping consistency.

3 Divide the mixture in half and spread it evenly into the prepared tins. Bake in the preheated oven for 25 minutes or until pale golden and soft and springy to the touch.

4 Remove from the oven and turn out on to a wire rack. Leave to cool. Carefully remove the lining paper and spread the base of one cake with the raspberry jam. Cover with the second cake layer, transfer to a plate and sprinkle the top with caster sugar to decorate.

 Oven temperature
180°C/350°F/gas 4

 Baking time
25 minutes

 Cake tins
Two 20cm (8in) Victoria Sandwich tins, greased and base-lined

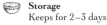 **Makes**
6–8 slices

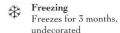 **Storage**
Keeps for 2–3 days

 Freezing
Freezes for 3 months, undecorated

Chiffon Cake

This is a close relation of Angel-food cake – a moist, light cake composed mostly of egg whites and sugar. For a Chiffon Cake, egg yolks and oil are included to give it a firmer structure and to enable it to take on flavours successfully, as in the Chocolate Mocha variation.

INGREDIENTS

180g (6oz) plain flour

2 tsp baking powder

250g (8oz) caster sugar

½ tsp salt

75ml (2½fl oz) corn or sunflower oil

5 egg yolks

125ml (4fl oz) cold water

1 tsp vanilla extract

1 tsp finely grated lemon zest

5 egg whites

½ tsp cream of tartar

icing sugar to decorate

1 Sift the flour, baking powder, sugar and salt together twice and then once more into a bowl. Make a well in the centre and add the oil, egg yolks, water, vanilla extract and lemon zest. Gradually whisk the dry ingredients into the liquid until the mixture is smooth and shiny.

2 In another bowl, whisk the egg whites and cream of tartar into soft peaks (see page 47). Gently fold into the main mixture a third at a time, taking care not to knock out the air.

Pour into the prepared tin and bake in the preheated oven for 1 hour or until a skewer inserted into the cake comes out clean.

3 Remove from the oven and invert straight on to a wire rack. Leave in the tin until cold. Carefully run a round-bladed knife around the sides of the tin and the central tube and turn out. Leave for 1 day before serving. Dust lightly with icing sugar to decorate.

VARIATIONS

Almond Chiffon Cake
Fold 100g (3½oz) ground almonds into the finished cake mixture. Bake as before.

Chocolate Mocha Chiffon Cake
Melt 90g (3oz) plain chocolate with 2 teaspoons instant coffee powder dissolved in 1 tablespoon boiling water (see page 44). Sift 1½ teaspoons ground cinnamon with the flour, baking powder, sugar and salt. Add the oil, egg yolks, water and vanilla. Omit the lemon zest. Beat together well and stir in the chocolate. Gently fold in the whisked egg whites and bake as before.

 Oven temperature
160°C/325°F/gas 3

 Baking time
1 hour

 Cake tin
24cm (9½in) Angel-food cake tin, spotlessly clean and dusted with flour

 Makes
12 slices

 Storage
Leave for 1 day before serving; keeps for 2–3 days

 Freezing
Freezes for 1–2 months

Rich Genoese Sponge

When butter is added to a fatless sponge it is known as a Genoese. The addition of butter improves the flavour of the cake and also enhances its keeping properties. Genoese Sponge also freezes well. Use unsalted butter, which has a sweeter flavour, never margarine. This is a richer version of a traditional Genoese, which usually has half this amount of butter.

INGREDIENTS

For the cake

125g (4oz) unsalted butter

125g (4oz) caster sugar

4 large eggs (size 1), separated

1 tsp finely grated lemon zest

125g (4oz) plain flour, sifted

For the filling and decoration

½ quantity lemon mousseline buttercream (see page 150)

icing sugar

1 For the cake, melt the butter in a small pan over a low heat. Remove from the heat and leave to cool.

2 Set aside 2 tablespoons of the caster sugar. Whisk the remaining sugar and the egg yolks together to the ribbon stage (see page 48), then whisk in the lemon zest.

3 In another bowl, whisk the egg whites into soft peaks (see page 47). Sprinkle over the reserved sugar and whisk until they form slightly stiffer peaks.

4 Carefully fold 2 large spoonfuls of the egg white into the egg yolk mixture to loosen the texture. Gently fold in the flour, followed by the melted butter, taking care not to add any of the milky liquid that collects in the bottom of the pan. Gently fold in the remaining egg whites, taking care not to knock out the air.

5 Pour the mixture into the prepared tin and bake in the preheated oven for about 45–50 minutes or until golden and a skewer inserted into the cake comes out clean.

6 Remove the cake from the oven and leave to rest in the tin for 5 minutes. Turn out on to a wire rack, peel off the lining paper and leave to cool.

7 Cut the cake horizontally in half. Sandwich together with the lemon buttercream. Transfer the cake to a serving plate and dust lightly with a little icing sugar to decorate.

 Oven temperature
180°C/350°F/gas 4

 Baking time
45–50 minutes

 Cake tin
22cm (8½in) springform tin, greased, floured and base-lined

 Makes
8 slices

 Storage
Keeps for 1 week

 Freezing
Freezes for 2–3 months, undecorated

 Step ahead
Make the lemon mousseline buttercream

Japanese Kastella

Although possibly the most popular cake in Japan today, Kastella originated in Portuguese Madeira, and is reputed to have been brought to the southern Japanese island of Kyusha in the 16th century. Traditionally, it is offered with a cup of green tea. As presentation and style are very important in Japanese culture, serve this cake in small slices on elegant plates, perhaps with whole strawberries on their stalks set alongside.

INGREDIENTS

6 egg yolks

100g (3½ oz) caster sugar

2 tsp honey

pinch of salt

75ml (5 tbsp) condensed milk

90g (3oz) plain flour, sifted

4 egg whites

icing sugar to decorate

1 Whisk the egg yolks and sugar together to the ribbon stage (see page 48). Whisk in the honey, salt and condensed milk.

2 Stir the flour into the egg yolk mixture. In another bowl, whisk the egg whites into soft peaks (see page 47). Stir 2 large spoonfuls of the whisked egg whites into the egg yolk mixture to loosen the texture. Carefully fold in the remaining egg white, taking care not to knock out the air.

3 Pour the mixture into the prepared tin and bake in the preheated oven for 45 minutes or until richly golden and a skewer inserted into the cake comes out clean.

4 Remove from the oven and leave to rest in the tin for 5 minutes. Turn out on to a wire rack, carefully peel off the lining paper and leave to cool.

5 To decorate, dust the top of the cake lightly with icing sugar just before serving.

 Oven temperature
160°C/325°F/gas 3

 Baking time
45 minutes

 Cake tin
22cm (8½in) springform tin, greased and base-lined

 Makes
16 slices

 Storage
Keeps for 2–3 days

 Freezing
Freezes for 2–3 months

Biscuit Roulade with Rice Flour

Rice flour has an almost nutty flavour and aroma. It makes a light and fluffy sponge that holds its shape when cool. A jam filling complements it well. Offer this cake to people who don't eat wheat and they will feel very spoiled.

INGREDIENTS

For the cake

6 eggs, separated

90g (3oz) caster sugar

75g (2½ oz) rice flour

For the filling and decoration

6–8 tbsp apricot or raspberry jam, sieved

caster sugar

1 For the cake, whisk the egg yolks and sugar together to the ribbon stage (see page 48).

2 In another bowl whisk the egg whites into soft peaks (see page 47). Gently fold the flour then the egg whites into the egg yolk mixture, taking care not to knock out the air.

3 Pour the mixture into the prepared tin. Lightly level the surface, making sure the corners are well filled. Bake in the centre of the preheated oven for 8 minutes or until soft and springy to the touch.

4 Remove the cake from the oven and turn out on to a sheet of silicone or greaseproof paper sprinkled with caster sugar. Peel off the lining paper.

5 Spread the surface of the sponge with the jam and then, starting with one short edge, roll up (see step 2 opposite). Leave to cool on a wire rack. Transfer to a plate and sprinkle with caster sugar.

 Oven temperature
230°C/450°F/gas 8

 Baking time
8 minutes

 Cake tin
36x25x1cm (14x10x½in) Swiss roll tin, greased and lined

 Makes
12–14 slices

Storage
Keeps for 2 days

Freezing
Freezes for 1–2 months

Piskóta with Walnuts

This sponge cake was brought into the Hungarian court of King Matthias in the late 15th century, after he married Princess Beatrix, the daughter of the King of Naples. This Piskóta is made as a roulade and flavoured with walnuts.

INGREDIENTS

For the cake

4 eggs, separated

75g (2½ oz) caster sugar

1 tsp instant coffee powder

2 tsp dark rum

90g (3oz) walnut pieces, finely chopped

For the filling

300ml (½ pint) double cream

1 tbsp dark rum

2 tbsp caster sugar

For the decoration

200g (7oz) plain chocolate

walnut pieces

1 For the cake, whisk the egg yolks and sugar together to the ribbon stage (see page 48). Dissolve the coffee powder in the rum and whisk into the egg yolk mixture.

2 In another bowl, whisk the egg whites into soft peaks (see page 47). Carefully fold the walnut pieces into the egg yolk mixture, followed by the egg whites, taking care not to knock out the air.

3 Pour the mixture into the prepared tin. Lightly level the surface, making sure the corners are well filled. Bake in the preheated oven for about 15–20 minutes or until lightly browned and soft and springy to the touch.

4 Remove from the oven and turn out on to a sheet of silicone paper sprinkled with caster sugar. Peel off the lining paper and cover with more silicone paper and a slightly damp tea towel. Leave to cool.

5 For the filling, whip the cream, dark rum and caster sugar into soft peaks and spread over the roulade, then roll up (see steps 1 and 2 opposite).

6 For the decoration, melt the chocolate (see page 44) then spread it evenly over the roulade with a palette knife. Leave to cool slightly then swirl gently with a fork (see step 3 opposite). Sprinkle over the walnut pieces and leave to set before serving.

 **Oven temperature**
180°C/350°F/gas 4

 Baking time
15–20 minutes

 **Cake tin**
36x25x1cm (14x10x½in) Swiss roll tin, greased and lined

 Makes
12 slices

 Storage
Keeps for 2–3 days

Filling and Rolling the Piskóta

1 Remove the tea towel and clean silicone or greaseproof paper. Spread the rum-flavoured cream over the Piskóta in an even layer to within 2.5cm (1in) of the edge.

2 Starting with one short edge, roll up the sponge using the paper to support and guide it. Place, seam-side down, on a wire rack set over a large baking tray or plate.

3 Pour the melted chocolate over the Piskóta and spread evenly over the cake's surface. Leave for a few minutes to cool slightly and then make swirls in the chocolate with a fork.

DECORATING THE PISKOTA
Sprinkle the chocolate surface of the cake with the walnut pieces and leave until set. Carefully transfer to a serving plate.

A delightful nutty sponge, filled with fresh cream

Luxury Layered Cakes

In the 19th century, cakes were influenced by the French chef Antonin Carême who, guided by his love of sculpture and architecture, created highly elaborate masterpieces. Luxury cakes today may not compare with such works of art, but richly decorated syrup-soaked sponges, crumbly pastries, fragile meringues and crisp choux puffs, filled with cream, chocolate, nuts and liqueurs, still make unrivalled centrepieces at the dinner table.

Esterházy Cream Torte

Layers of light almond cake are sandwiched together with a creamy and mildly alcoholic filling. Toasted almonds decorate the sides and add a delicate crunch. This cake is mouthwatering, rich and always impressive.

A crown of fresh, sugar-frosted grapes

Special Ingredients

Lemon peel *flavours the almond sponge.*

Almonds *add a buttery character to the cake.*

Grapes *introduce a fresh flavour and smooth texture.*

Gelatine *stabilizes and firmly sets the frothy wine and cream filling.*

Sweet white wines *like Marsala have full-bodied flavours.*

Dark rum *gives both depth and richness of flavour to the sweet wine in the cream layer.*

Making the Cake

An Austrian recipe of 1899 named in honour of the princely Magyar family Esterházy. Egg yolks, sugar and a sweet, quality wine are whipped over heat into a type of zabaglione; cream and rum are added and the blend of flavours combined with the almond sponge is splendid.

INGREDIENTS

For the cake

1 quantity Whipped Almond Cake (see page 105)

For the filling

3 tbsp water

1 tbsp gelatine powder

300ml (½ pint) double cream

2 tbsp dark rum

4 egg yolks

125g (4oz) caster sugar

150ml (¼ pint) sweet white wine, such as Marsala or Sauternes

For the decoration

450ml (¾ pint) double cream, whipped

125g (4oz) toasted flaked almonds

2–3 tbsp icing sugar

180g (6oz) frosted green grapes (see page 148)

1 Make the almond cake in the prepared 24cm (9½in) tin (see page 105). Bake in the preheated oven for 1 hour and leave to cool. Cut horizontally into two layers and place the bottom half into the base of the prepared 22cm (8½in) tin.

2 For the filling, put the water into a small bowl, sprinkle over the gelatine and leave for 5 minutes. Sit the bowl in a pan of simmering water and leave until clear (see page 45). Remove and leave to cool slightly. Whip the cream with the rum into soft peaks. Set aside.

3 Put the egg yolks and sugar into a large heatproof bowl. Whisk until pale and creamy. Add the wine, rest the bowl over a large pan of simmering water and whisk until the mixture is thick and mousse-like. Take the pan off the heat, and continue whisking over the water until the mixture has thickened even more. Lift off the bowl and place it in a larger bowl filled with iced cold water. Whisk until the mixture reaches the ribbon stage (see page 48) and is cool.

4 Slowly whisk the dissolved gelatine into the mousse mixture. Gently fold in the rum-flavoured whipped cream. Set aside a quarter of the mixture. Pour the remainder into the tin and cover with the top layer of the cake. Spread the remaining mixture over the top of the cake and chill for 3–4 hours until set.

5 Remove the cake from the tin and transfer to a plate. For the decoration, spoon a quarter of the whipped cream into a piping bag fitted with a 1cm (½in) star nozzle. Spread the rest around the side of the cake and press on the almonds (see page 143). Mark a diamond pattern on top with a knife and dust well with icing sugar. Pipe small stars of cream (see page 145) around the top edge of the cake and finish with the grapes.

 Oven temperature
160°C/325°F/gas 3

Baking time
1 hour

Cake tins
One 24cm (9½in) springform tin, greased and base-lined for the cake; one 22cm (8½in) springform tin, lightly oiled, in which to assemble the torte

Makes
12 slices

Storage
Keeps for 2–3 days

Step ahead
Make the almond cake; prepare the frosted grapes

Mozart Torte

Wolfgang Amadeus Mozart is the inspiration for this lovely dessert. A delicate almond and apricot sponge is soaked with Cointreau-flavoured syrup and then layered with an almond Japonais. It is finished with a thick coating of chocolate ganache, then a layer of whipped cream.

INGREDIENTS

For the base

½ quantity Japonais mixture (see page 117) made with ground almonds

For the cake

90g (3oz) ground almonds

100g (3½ oz) icing sugar, sifted

4 egg whites

5 egg yolks

pinch of salt

1 tbsp water

2 tsp finely grated lemon zest

100g (3½ oz) caster sugar

2 tbsp cornflour, sifted

60g (2oz) plain flour, sifted

150g (5oz) canned or bottled apricots, drained and chopped

30g (1oz) butter, melted and cooled slightly

For the filling and decoration

1 quantity chocolate ganache (see page 151)

4 tbsp Cointreau-flavoured syrup (see page 155)

300ml (½ pint) double cream

chocolate curls (see page 147)

1 For the base, make the Japonais mixture with ground almonds instead of ground hazelnuts (see page 117). Spread evenly on to the base of the prepared tin and bake in the preheated oven for 1 hour. Remove from the oven and leave in the tin on a wire rack to cool. Turn out of the tin and peel off the lining paper. Wash and re-line the tin. Raise the oven temperature.

2 For the cake, put the almonds and icing sugar together into a large bowl. Stir in 1 egg white to make a smooth, stiff paste. Beat in the egg yolks, one at a time, followed by the salt, water and lemon zest.

3 In another bowl, whisk the remaining egg whites into stiff peaks. Gradually whisk in half the caster sugar until they form a stiff, glossy meringue (see page 49). Gently fold in the remaining caster sugar and the sifted cornflour.

4 Gently fold the flour into the almond mixture, followed by the apricots and melted butter, taking care not to add any of the milky liquid that collects in the bottom of the pan. Fold 2 large spoonfuls of the meringue into the almond mixture to loosen the texture, then carefully fold in the remainder, until everything is evenly mixed.

5 Pour the mixture into the prepared tin and lightly level the surface. Bake in the preheated oven for 50 minutes or until golden and a skewer inserted into the cake comes out clean. Leave to rest in the tin for 10 minutes. Turn out on to a wire rack, carefully peel off the lining paper and leave to cool.

TO FINISH THE CAKE

1 Place the Japonais layer on a serving plate and spread with a 5mm (¼ in) thick layer of the chocolate ganache. Cover with the almond and apricot sponge. Sprinkle the surface of the sponge evenly with the Cointreau-flavoured syrup and leave for 5–10 minutes to allow the syrup to soak in.

2 Spread the remaining ganache over the top and sides of the cake in an even layer (see page 142). Chill for 1 hour or until the ganache has set.

3 Whip the cream into stiff peaks. Carefully spread it evenly over the top and sides of the cake using a palette knife, making sure that none of the chocolate ganache shows through. Sprinkle the top of the cake generously with chocolate curls to decorate. Chill overnight before serving.

Oven temperature
160°C/325°F/gas 3 for the Japonais base; 180°C/350°F/gas 4 for the cake

Baking time
1 hour for the Japonais base; 50 minutes for the cake

Cake tin
22cm (8½ in) springform tin, greased and base-lined

Makes
12–16 slices

Storage
Chill overnight before serving; keeps for 3 days

Step ahead
Make the chocolate ganache and Cointreau-flavoured syrup

Rum & Citrus Torte

A rich torte, this is typical of those popular in 19th-century Austria and Germany, usually flavoured with alcohol. Here, the whole cake is coated with a lemon-flavoured glacé icing and decorated with pistachio nuts and curls of coarse orange and lemon zest. (See page 13 for illustration.)

INGREDIENTS

For the cake
1 quantity Biscuit de Savoie sponge mixture (see page 65)

1 tsp finely grated orange zest

1 tsp finely grated lemon zest

For the filling
3 egg whites

150g (5oz) icing sugar

250g (8oz) unsalted butter, softened

1 tbsp dark rum

1 tbsp finely grated orange zest

orange and green liquid food colouring (optional)

3 tbsp blanched pistachio nuts (see page 45), finely chopped

135ml (9 tbsp) rum and citrus-flavoured syrup (see page 155)

For the decoration
60–75ml (4–5 tbsp) apricot glaze (see page 149)

2 quantities lemon glacé icing (see page 152)

30g (1oz) blanched pistachio nuts (see page 45), halved

coarse strands of orange and lemon zest (see page 149)

1 Make the cake mixture (see page 65), adding the orange and lemon zest to the whisked egg yolks and sugar. Pour the mixture equally into the prepared tins and bake in the preheated oven for 20 minutes or until a skewer inserted into each of the cakes comes out clean. Remove from the oven and leave to rest in the tins for 5–10 minutes. Turn out on to a wire rack and leave to cool. Peel off the lining paper.

2 For the filling, put the egg whites and sugar together into a large, heatproof bowl. Rest over a large pan of simmering water and whisk vigorously for 3 minutes or until they form a stiff meringue. Take the pan off the heat and whisk for another 1–2 minutes. Transfer the mixture to a cold bowl and leave to cool.

3 In another bowl, beat the butter until pale and fluffy. Gradually beat in the meringue mixture, one spoonful at a time, until well combined. Slowly beat in the rum.

4 Spoon a third of the mixture into another bowl and beat in the orange zest and a little orange food colouring if using. Stir the pistachio nuts and a little green food colouring, if using, into the larger amount. Cover both bowls with clingfilm and chill for 15 minutes.

TO FINISH THE CAKE

1 Slice each cake horizontally in half. Sprinkle the cut side of each layer evenly with one quarter of the rum and citrus-flavoured syrup. Leave to stand for 5–10 minutes to allow the syrup to soak in.

2 Place the bottom layer of one cake on a board and spread with half the pistachio buttercream. Cover with the next cake layer and spread over the orange buttercream. Cover with the bottom layer of the second cake and spread with the remaining pistachio buttercream. Cover with the remaining cake layer. Press the layers together to bind well and then tidy up the side of the cake to give a smooth surface (see page 52).

3 Place the cake on a wire rack set over a plate. Brush the top and sides of the cake with the apricot glaze and leave for 5 minutes to set.

4 To decorate, pour the glacé icing on to the cake and coax evenly over the top and sides with a palette knife (see page 142). Sprinkle the top with the halved pistachio nuts and the strands of orange and lemon zest and leave to set. Transfer the cake to a plate and leave overnight before serving.

 Oven temperature
180°C/350°F/gas 4

 Baking time
20 minutes

 Cake tins
Two 22cm (8½in) springform tins, greased and base-lined

 Makes
8–10 slices

Storage
Leave overnight before serving; keeps for 4–5 days

Dobos Torta

The Hungarian pastry chef József C. Dobos created this lovely torta in 1906 and donated the recipe to the local Pastry and Honey-Breadmakers Guild. Layers of sponge are sandwiched together with a rich chocolate buttercream, and the whole cake is topped with distinctive honey-brown wedges of caramel. (See page 12 for illustration.)

INGREDIENTS

For the cake

75g (2½ oz) plain flour
75g (2½ oz) potato flour
150g (5oz) caster sugar
6 eggs, separated
1 tsp finely grated lemon or orange zest

For the filling and decoration

3 quantities quick chocolate buttercream (see page 151)
1 tsp butter
180g (6oz) granulated sugar
5 drops of lemon juice

1 For the cake, sift together the plain and potato flour and set aside. Set aside two thirds of the caster sugar. Whisk the egg yolks with the remaining sugar to the ribbon stage (see page 48). Whisk in the citrus zest.

2 In another bowl, whisk the egg whites into soft peaks. Gradually whisk in the reserved sugar to form stiff, glossy peaks (see page 49). Stir 2 large spoonfuls of the egg white into the egg yolk mixture to loosen the texture. Gently fold in the flour, followed by the remaining egg whites, taking care not to knock out the air.

3 Divide one third of the cake mixture between the two prepared tins. Spread in an even layer over the base of each one using the back of a spoon. Bake in the preheated oven for 5–6 minutes until lightly golden.

4 Remove the cakes from the oven and loosen the edges of each one with a small palette knife. Carefully turn out on to wire racks, peel off the lining paper and cover with clean sheets of silicone paper. Leave to cool. Re-line the tins and repeat the process twice more with the remaining mixture to make another four thin layers of sponge, making six in total.

TO FINISH THE CAKE

1 Set aside one quarter of the quick chocolate buttercream. Sandwich each of the six sponge layers together with a 5mm (¼ in) thick layer of the buttercream (see page 52), then spread more buttercream evenly over the top and sides of the cake (see page 142). Chill for 1 hour before decorating.

2 For the caramel decoration, draw a 22cm (8½ in) circle on a sheet of silicone paper. Mark it into eight or twelve even-sized wedges. Melt the butter in a heavy-based pan. Add the sugar and the lemon juice and heat gently, stirring now and then, until a golden caramel has formed.

3 Pour the caramel into the centre of the marked circle and quickly spread it out using a hot, clean palette knife. Leave for a few seconds until it is just starting to set. Then cut into eight or twelve wedges, using the marked lines as a guide, with a large, lightly greased, sharp knife. Remember to re-grease the knife with butter between each cut. Leave the caramel to cool and harden.

4 Spoon the reserved buttercream into a piping bag fitted with a 1cm (½ in) star nozzle. Pipe eight or twelve large rosettes (see page 145) at even intervals around the top edge of the cake. Rest a caramel wedge at an angle on each one.

Oven temperature
220°C/425°F/gas 7

Baking time
5–6 minutes for each batch

Cake tins
Two 22cm (8½ in) Victoria Sandwich tins, greased and base-lined

Makes
8–12 slices

Storage
Keeps for 4–5 days in a cool place; do not refrigerate

Step ahead
Make the quick chocolate buttercream

Hazelnut Macaroon Cake

This is probably the dessert that inspires the most effusive compliments of all; and it is quite irresistible. Four deliciously crunchy hazelnut-meringue layers are luxuriously sandwiched with a plain disc of meringue and filled with a luscious chocolate cream ganache.

INGREDIENTS

For the meringue layers

1 quantity Simple Meringues (see page 112)

6 egg whites

375g (12oz) caster sugar

375g (12oz) roasted hazelnuts (see page 45), finely ground

4 tsp cocoa powder

For the filling and decoration

3 quantities chocolate ganache (see page 151)

chocolate curls (see page 147)

1 Make the Simple Meringues mixture and spread it into the prepared tin. Bake in the preheated oven for 1½ hours or until crisp and dry. Remove from the oven, loosen the edges with a palette knife, lift out of the tin and leave to cool on a wire rack.

2 Whisk 3 of the egg whites into soft peaks. Gradually whisk in half the sugar to form a stiff, glossy meringue (see page 49). Mix half the hazelnuts with 2 teaspoons of the cocoa and gently fold in. Spoon the mixture on to the prepared baking sheets and spread out evenly within the marked circles (see page 49).

3 Bake in the preheated oven for 1 hour or until crisp and dry. Remove from the oven and leave to cool on wire racks. Re-line the baking sheets and repeat the process with the rest of the ingredients to make two more discs. Peel off the lining paper once the meringues are cold.

4 To assemble the cake, set aside half the ganache. Use the rest to sandwich together the meringue discs, with the plain disc in the centre. Spoon one third of the reserved ganache into a piping bag fitted with a 5mm (¼in) plain nozzle. Spread the rest over the top and sides of the cake (see page 142). Mark the sides with a confectionery comb (see page 143).

5 Mark the top of the cake into twelve wedges. Pipe beads of ganache around the base and top of the cake, then along the marked lines. Fill each segment with the chocolate curls. Chill for 2 hours before serving.

 Oven temperature
140°C/275°F/gas 1

 Baking time
1½ hours for the plain meringue; 1 hour for the hazelnut-meringue discs

 Cake tins
23cm (9in) springform tin, greased with oil and base-lined; two flat baking sheets, lined with silicone paper and marked with 23cm (9in) circles

 Makes
12 slices

 Storage
Keeps for 3 days in the refrigerator

 Freezing
Freezes for 1–2 months

 Step ahead
Prepare the roasted hazelnuts; make the chocolate ganache

Gâteau Saint Honoré

This cake is named after the patron saint of pastry cooks and bakers. A crown of choux pastry, made with milk and water to give a soft crust, is baked on to a shortcrust pastry base and filled with crème pâtissière. On to the crown is set a circlet of small caramelized choux pastry puffs. Assemble and finish this cake no more than 2–3 hours before serving.

INGREDIENTS

1 quantity pâte sucrée pastry (see page 55)

For the choux pastry

1 quantity choux pastry made with 125ml (4fl oz) each milk and water (see page 57)

1 egg yolk

For the caramel glaze

200g (7oz) granulated sugar

3 tbsp water

For the filling

150ml (¼ pint) double cream

2 tsp caster sugar

2 quantities crème pâtissière (see page 151)

1 Allow the pâte sucrée pastry to come back to room temperature. Knead briefly until smooth and then roll out on a lightly floured surface into a 23cm (9in) circle. Place on the greased baking sheet, prick all over with a fork and chill until ready to use.

2 Make the choux pastry. Spoon into a piping bag fitted with a 1cm (½in) plain nozzle. Mix the remaining beaten egg left over from making the choux pastry with the egg yolk and use a little to brush a 2.5cm (1in) strip around the edge of the chilled pastry circle. Pipe some of the choux pastry in a raised, thick band around the outside edge of the pastry.

3 Pipe the remaining choux pastry into 14–16 small 2.5cm (1in) mounds on the wet baking sheet (see page 57). Brush both these puffs and the choux pastry ring with the remaining beaten egg mixture.

4 Bake the choux puffs in the preheated oven for about 20 minutes or until crisp and golden. Remove from the oven and pierce a hole in the bottom of each one with a fine metal skewer. Return the puffs to the oven, upside down, for 5 minutes. Transfer the puffs to a wire rack and leave to cool.

5 Bake the pastry and choux base in the preheated oven for 10 minutes. Lower the oven temperature and cook for a further 20 minutes or until both the pastry base and the choux circle are golden brown. Remove from the oven, prick the choux pastry in several places to release the steam and return to the oven for 5 minutes. Transfer to a wire rack and leave to cool.

TO FINISH THE CAKE

1 Make the caramel glaze (see page 153). As soon as the syrup is amber-coloured, plunge the base of the pan into cold water to stop it from cooking further. Set aside in a bowl of very hot water to keep the caramel liquid. Carefully dip the top of each choux puff into the caramel (see step 1 opposite), place in a single layer on a wire rack, caramel side up, and leave to set.

2 For the filling, whip the cream and sugar together into stiff peaks. Spoon into a piping bag fitted with a 5mm (¼in) plain nozzle. Pipe into each puff through the hole in the base (see step 2 opposite).

3 If the caramel has set, place the pan over a low heat and heat gently until it is liquid again. Holding the top of each puff, quickly dip the base into the caramel and arrange side by side around the top of the choux ring (see step 3 opposite). Transfer the gâteau to a serving plate.

4 Spoon the crème pâtissière into a piping bag fitted with a 1cm (½in) star nozzle. Pipe in a rope design (see page 145) into the centre of the gâteau. Chill for 1 hour or until ready to serve.

Oven temperature
200°C/400°F/gas 6, then 190°C/375°F/gas 5

Baking time
25 minutes for the choux puffs; 35 minutes for the pastry and choux base

Cake tins
Two large, flat baking sheets, lightly greased; one run under cold water and left slightly wet

Makes
6–8 slices

Storage
Best eaten within 2–3 hours of assembly

Step ahead
Make the pâte sucrée pastry and crème pâtissière a day ahead; make the choux pastry a few hours beforehand

Glazing Choux Puffs

The finished gâteau

1 Spear each choux puff with the tip of a small sharp knife. Dip the top into the caramel and leave to set.

2 Pipe the whipped cream into each choux puff through the hole in the base, until it feels firm and full.

3 Dip the base of each puff quickly into the caramel and arrange side by side around the top of the choux ring.

The piped crème pâtissière gives a decorative finish

Chocolate Cakes

Nothing inspires descriptive indulgence quite as much as chocolate: "Pure, delicious, refreshing, stimulating, light and refined", so the words of an early 20th-century advertisment pointed out, defining its great medicinal virtues. The best chocolate cakes excite the taste buds with the suggestion of luscious and warming sweetness, and entice both the palate and the eye. Chocolate combined with different blends of nuts and seeds, fruit, creams, coffee and spices, and spirits and liqueurs becomes wickedly sinful and delicious, and an absolute joy to eat.

Sour Cherry & Chocolate Torte

The layered combination of black cherries, Kirsch, chocolate and cream has long been popular in the dessert repertoire. Here is a more unusual variation using a crunchy hazelnut Japonais layer in the middle of more traditional chocolate layers. For a very simple cake, the basic chocolate sponge can be sandwiched together with whipped cream or chocolate buttercream.

INGREDIENTS

For the cake

1 tsp instant coffee powder
1½ tbsp boiling water
45g (1½ oz) plain chocolate
90g (3oz) plain flour, sifted
1 tbsp cocoa powder
½ tsp ground cinnamon
3 eggs, separated
90g (3oz) light muscovado sugar
90g (3oz) unsalted butter, melted and cooled
½ quantity Japonais mixture (see page 117)

For the filling and decoration

900ml (1½ pints) double cream
6 tbsp caster sugar
4 tbsp dark rum or Kirsch
90ml (6 tbsp) Kirsch-flavoured syrup (see page 155)
750g (1½ lb) fresh cherries, stoned
75g (2½ oz) plain chocolate, coarsely grated (see page 147)
1 quantity chocolate caraque (see page 146)
12 fresh cherries with leaves

1 For the cake, dissolve the coffee in the water then melt with the chocolate (see page 44). Leave to cool. Sift together the flour, cocoa and cinnamon.

2 Whisk the egg yolks and sugar until fluffy. Stir in the chocolate. Whisk the egg whites into soft peaks. Stir 2 spoonfuls into the egg yolk mixture to loosen the texture. Fold in the flour, butter and remaining egg whites until evenly mixed.

3 Spoon the mixture into the prepared tin and bake in the preheated oven for 25 minutes. Remove from the oven and leave in the tin for 5 minutes. Turn out on to a wire rack, peel off the lining paper and leave to cool. Re-line the tin and lower the oven temperature.

4 Make the Japonais (see page 117). Spread into the tin and bake for 1 hour. Remove from the oven and leave to cool.

TO FINISH THE CAKE
1 Whip the cream, sugar and rum or Kirsch into soft peaks. Set aside two thirds. Slice the cake horizontally in half and sprinkle each layer with syrup. Place half the cherries on the bottom layer, then spread with half the remaining cream. Cover with the Japonais. Scatter over the remaining cherries, spread with the rest of the cream and cover with the top cake layer.

2 Spread two thirds of reserved cream over the cake. Coat the sides with the grated chocolate (see page 143). Spoon the rest of the cream into a piping bag fitted with a 1cm (½in) star nozzle and pipe shells around the top (see page 145). Finish with caraque and cherries. Chill for 3–4 hours.

Oven temperature
180°C/350°F/gas 4 for the cake;
160°C/325°F/gas 3 for the Japonais

Baking time
25 minutes for the cake;
1 hour for the Japonais

Cake tin
22cm (8½in) Victoria Sandwich tin, greased and base-lined

Makes
12–16 slices

Storage
Keeps for 3–4 days in the refrigerator

Freezing
Freezes for 1–2 months, undecorated

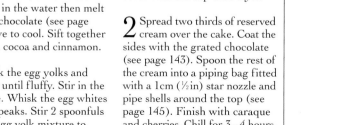

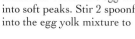

Special Ingredients

Plain chocolate should contain at least 70% cocoa solids for the richest flavour.

Hazelnuts, lightly roasted, add texture and flavour to the Japonais layer.

Fresh cherries taste best. Use canned or bottled cherries if fresh are unavailable.

Cocoa is cheaper than chocolate and gives depth of flavour to the sponge.

Cinnamon has a sweet, woody and intense aroma that enhances chocolate well.

Dark rum adds a mellow note and gives a punch to the chocolate layers.

Fresh cream piped in a shell design

Fresh cherries, cherry leaves and chocolate caraque make a stunning decoration

Chocolate Truffle Torte

This is a moist, rich cake that might have been especially developed for "chocoholics". Assemble it at least a day before it is needed so that the flavours have time to blend.

INGREDIENTS

For the cake

2 quantities chocolate cake mixture (see Sour Cherry & Chocolate Torte page 78)

For the truffles

2 tsp instant coffee powder
2 tbsp Tia Maria
125g (4oz) plain chocolate
60g (2oz) unsalted butter
2 tbsp icing sugar, sifted
1 tbsp double cream
5–4 tbsp cocoa powder

For the filling and decoration

150ml (¼ pint) double cream
2 tsp caster sugar
1 tbsp Tia Maria or dark rum
90ml (6 tbsp) Tia Maria-flavoured syrup (see page 155)
2 quantities quick chocolate buttercream (see page 151)

1 Make the chocolate cake mixture (see page 78). Divide between the prepared tins and bake in the preheated oven for 25 minutes or until a skewer inserted into each cake comes out clean. Remove from the oven and leave to cool on a wire rack. Turn out of the tins and peel off the lining paper.

2 For the truffles, dissolve the coffee in the Tia Maria. Melt the chocolate with the dissolved coffee (see page 44). Leave to cool. Beat the butter and sugar together. Beat in the chocolate mixture and the cream. Chill for 40 minutes. Shape the mixture into 14 even-sized balls, toss in the cocoa powder and chill for 2 hours (see steps 1–3 below).

3 For the filling, whip the cream, sugar and Tia Maria into stiff peaks. Cover and chill.

TO FINISH THE CAKE

1 Slice each cake horizontally in half and sprinkle each cut side with one quarter of the Tia Maria-flavoured syrup.

2 Spoon one quarter of the chocolate buttercream into a piping bag fitted with a 1cm (½in) star nozzle. Reserve half the remainder. Set both aside.

3 Sandwich together the cake layers in pairs using the rest of the buttercream (see page 52). Sandwich these together with the whipped cream.

4 For the decoration, spread the reserved buttercream over the cake (see page 142). Pipe 14 rosettes of buttercream around the top edge (see page 145) and rest a truffle on each. Chill overnight before serving.

 Oven temperature
180°C/350°F/gas 4

 Baking time
25 minutes

 Cake tins
Two 22cm (8½in) Victoria Sandwich tins, greased and base-lined

 Makes
14 slices

 Storage
Leave for 1 day before serving; keeps for 1 week

❄ **Freezing**
Freezes for 1–2 months

Step ahead
Make the truffles and chill for 2 hours; make the Tia Maria-flavoured syrup and the quick chocolate buttercream

Making Chocolate Truffles

1 *Divide the mixture into 14 pieces. Lightly roll each piece between your fingers, having dusted them first with a little cocoa powder. If the balls are soft, chill them until firm.*

2 *To coat the truffles, sift the cocoa powder into a medium-sized bowl. Drop in three truffles at a time and gently swirl the bowl until each one is evenly coated.*

3 *Carefully lift the truffles out of the bowl and lay them, spaced a little apart, on a baking tray lined with silicone paper. Chill for 2 hours or until firm.*

Orange & Chocolate Layer Cake

Containing just a hint of chocolate blended with almond, this fine-textured cake is quite light in colour. The tang of the orange in the buttercream filling provides a delicious contrast.

INGREDIENTS

For the cake

90g (3oz) caster sugar

6 eggs, separated

60g (2oz) light muscovado sugar

60g (2oz) plain flour

4 tbsp drinking chocolate powder

100g (3½ oz) ground almonds

15g (½oz) unsalted butter, melted

For the filling and decoration

2½ quantities orange mousseline buttercream (see page 150)

10–12 chocolate fans (see page 145)

1 For the cake, set aside 2 tablespoons of the caster sugar. Whisk the egg yolks, remaining caster sugar and muscovado sugar together until thick and mousse-like.

2 Sift the flour and drinking chocolate powder together twice. Gently fold into the egg yolk mixture, followed by the ground almonds and the melted butter, taking care not to add any of the milky liquid that collects in the bottom of the pan.

3 In another bowl, whisk the egg whites into soft peaks (see page 47). Whisk in the reserved sugar. Stir 2 large spoonfuls into the main mixture to loosen the texture, then gently fold in the remainder, taking care not to knock out the air.

4 Pour the mixture into the prepared tins and bake in the preheated oven for about 25 minutes or until a skewer inserted into each cake comes out clean. Remove from the oven and leave to rest in the tins for 5 minutes. Turn out, peel off the lining paper and leave to cool on a wire rack.

TO FINISH THE CAKE

1 Slice each cake horizontally in half. Spoon one fifth of the buttercream into a piping bag fitted with a 1cm (½in) star nozzle. Sandwich the cake layers together with half the remaining buttercream.

2 Spread the rest of the buttercream over the top and sides of the cake. Mark the sides into lines with a confectionery comb (see page 143). Carefully pipe the reserved buttercream in a rope design around the top of the cake (see page 145) and decorate with chocolate fans.

Oven temperature
180°C/350°F/gas 4

Baking time
25 minutes

Cake tins
Two 22cm (8½in) springform tins, greased and base-lined

Makes
16 slices

Storage
Keeps for 3–4 days

Freezing
Freezes for 1–2 months, undecorated

Step ahead
Make the orange mousseline buttercream and the chocolate fans

---

Fudge Squares

These squares are very easy to make. All the ingredients are simply mixed together in one large bowl with an electric mixer. The finished texture of the cake is very rich and fudgy.

INGREDIENTS

250g (8oz) plain chocolate

125g (4oz) butter, softened and cut into small pieces

4 eggs, lightly beaten

150g (5oz) caster sugar

75g (2½ oz) self-raising flour, sifted

icing sugar to decorate

1 Melt the chocolate in a small heatproof bowl (see page 44) and leave to cool. Put the butter, eggs, caster sugar and flour together in a large bowl. Add the cooled chocolate and beat together slowly until everything is evenly mixed.

2 Continue to beat the mixture more quickly for about 10 minutes until it has thickened, increased in volume and become much paler in colour.

3 Pour the mixture carefully into the prepared tin and bake in the preheated oven for about 1 hour or until a skewer inserted into the centre of the cake comes out clean.

4 Remove from the oven and leave to cool on a wire rack. Turn out of the tin, peel off the lining paper and cut evenly into squares. Dust with icing sugar.

Oven temperature
180°C/350°F/gas 4

Baking time
1 hour

Cake tin
22cm (8½in) square tin, greased and base-lined

Makes
16–24 squares

Storage
Keep for 4–5 days

Freezing
Freeze for 1–2 months

Chocolate Chestnut Roulade

A soft Swiss roll with a difference. Almonds lend bite to this mixture and butter moistness, so the cake can be rolled up when cold.

INGREDIENTS

For the cake

90g (3oz) plain chocolate

4 eggs, separated

30g (1oz) caster sugar

1 tbsp icing sugar

45g (1½ oz) unblanched almonds, very finely chopped

45g (1½ oz) butter, melted and cooled

For the filling and decoration

2 tsp cocoa powder

1 tsp icing sugar

1 quantity chestnut buttercream (see page 130)

150ml (¼ pint) double cream, whipped

chocolate curls (see page 147)

3 marrons glacés, halved

1 For the cake, melt the chocolate (see page 44) and leave to cool. Whisk the egg yolks and caster sugar together to the ribbon stage (see page 48).

2 In another bowl, whisk the egg whites into soft peaks (see page 47). Sift over the icing sugar and whisk until they form slightly stiffer peaks. Stir the chocolate, almonds and butter into the egg yolk mixture. Gently fold in the egg whites, taking care not to knock out the air.

3 Pour the mixture into the prepared tin and level the surface. Bake in the preheated oven for 15–20 minutes until soft and springy to the touch. Remove from the oven and cover with silicone paper and a damp tea towel. Leave to cool.

4 Sift the cocoa and icing sugar on to more silicone paper. Uncover the roulade and turn it out on to the paper. Peel off the lining paper and spread over the buttercream to within 1cm (½in) of the edge (see page 53). Roll up from one short edge, then place seam-side down on a plate.

5 Spoon the cream into a piping bag fitted with a 1cm (½in) star nozzle. Pipe a scroll down the centre of the cake (see page 145). Finish with chocolate curls and marrons glacés.

 Oven temperature
180°C/350°F/gas 4

 Baking time
15–20 minutes

 Cake tin
36x25x1cm (14x10x½in) Swiss roll tin, greased and lined

 Makes
12 slices

 Storage
Keeps for 3–4 days

 Freezing
Freezes for 1 month, undecorated

 Step ahead
Make the chestnut buttercream

Warning
This recipe contains raw eggs (see page 9)

Moist Chocolate & Hazelnut Cake

My sister Annette loves to bake and this recipe, my brother-in-law's absolute favourite, is from her repertoire. The cake is made without flour.

INGREDIENTS

For the cake

180g (6oz) plain chocolate

180g (6oz) caster sugar

180g (6oz) butter

6 eggs, separated

180g (6oz) roasted hazelnuts, ground

For the decoration

2 tbsp apricot glaze (see page 149)

100g (3½ oz) plain chocolate

1 tbsp butter

2 tbsp water

chopped roasted hazelnuts

1 Melt the chocolate (see page 44) and leave to cool. Beat all but 3 tablespoons sugar with the butter until pale and fluffy. Mix in the egg yolks and chocolate.

2 In another bowl, whisk the egg whites into soft peaks. Whisk in the reserved sugar. Stir 2 spoonfuls into the main mixture. Gently fold in the nuts and remaining egg whites.

3 Pour the mixture into the prepared tin and bake in the preheated oven for 45–55 minutes or until a skewer comes out clean. Remove from the oven and leave for 5 minutes. Turn out on to a wire rack and peel off the lining paper. Brush the top with the glaze and leave to cool.

4 Melt the chocolate with the butter and water. Pour on to the cake and spread over the top and sides. Sprinkle with the chopped nuts and leave to set.

 Oven temperature
180°C/350°F/gas 4

 Baking time
45–55 minutes

 Cake tin
23cm (9in) springform tin, greased and lined

 Makes
12 slices

 Storage
Keeps for 1 week

 Freezing
Freezes for 1–2 months, undecorated

Step ahead
Prepare the roasted hazelnuts (see page 45)

Nutty Brownies

Brownies must always be dense, dark, soft and fudgy, studded with nuts and full of rich chocolate.

INGREDIENTS

60g (2oz) plain chocolate

125g (4oz) butter

60g (2oz) plain flour

pinch of salt

2 eggs

175g (6oz) dark muscovado sugar

½ tsp vanilla extract

125g (4oz) walnuts or pecan nuts, coarsely chopped

1 Melt the chocolate with the butter (see page 44) and leave to cool. Sift together the flour and salt and set aside.

2 In another bowl, whisk the eggs and sugar together to the ribbon stage (see page 48). Stir in the melted chocolate and the vanilla extract.

3 Gently fold alternating spoonfuls of the flour and the chopped nuts into the main mixture, until everything is evenly mixed.

4 Pour the mixture into the prepared tin and bake in the preheated oven for 25 minutes until the top is shiny and firm but the centre is still slightly soft. Remove from the oven and leave in the tin on a wire rack to cool. Turn out of the tin, peel off the lining paper and cut into even-sized squares to serve.

Oven temperature
180°C/350°F/gas 4

Baking time
25 minutes

Cake tin
20cm (8in) shallow square tin, greased and base-lined

Makes
9–12 squares

Storage
Keep for 1 week

Freezing
Freeze for 1–2 months

Sacher Torte

A variation of the classic Viennese confection created by Franz Sacher in 1832 for Prince Metternich. The original recipe has been kept a closely guarded secret and is still the subject of litigation – but it is probably the most famous chocolate cake in the world. (See page 15 for illustration.)

INGREDIENTS

For the cake

125g (4oz) plain chocolate

100g (3½oz) icing sugar, sifted

100g (3½oz) unsalted butter

5 egg yolks

½ tsp vanilla extract

4 egg whites

100g (3½oz) ground almonds

3 tbsp plain flour, sifted

For the decoration

2 tbsp apricot glaze (see page 149)

1 quantity rich chocolate icing (see page 147)

chocolate leaves (see page 146)

1 For the cake, melt the chocolate (see page 44) and leave to cool slightly. Reserve 2 tablespoons of the icing sugar. Beat the remainder with the butter until pale and fluffy. Beat in the egg yolks, one at a time. Stir in the vanilla and chocolate.

2 In another bowl, whisk the egg whites into soft peaks. Whisk in the reserved sugar. Stir 2 large spoonfuls into the main mixture to loosen the texture.

3 Fold in alternating spoonfuls of almonds and flour. Gently fold in the remaining egg whites, until everything is evenly mixed.

4 Pour the mixture into the prepared tin and lightly level the surface. Rap the tin once on the work surface to disperse any pockets of air that might be trapped in the mixture.

5 Bake in the preheated oven for 45–50 minutes or until a skewer inserted into the cake comes out clean. Remove from the oven and leave to rest in the tin for 10 minutes. Turn out on to a wire rack, peel off the lining paper and leave to cool.

6 For the decoration, brush the top and sides of the cake with the apricot glaze. Place on a wire rack set over a plate and pour on the rich chocolate icing. If necessary, tilt the cake so that the icing coats the top and sides evenly (see page 147). Transfer to a plate and arrange the chocolate leaves around the edge of the cake to decorate. Leave to set before serving.

Oven temperature
180°C/350°F/gas 4

Baking time
45–50 minutes

Cake tin
22cm (8½in) springform tin, greased and base-lined

Makes
12–16 slices

Storage
Keeps for 4–5 days

Freezing
Freezes for 1–2 months, undecorated

Chocolate Fudge Cake

If you have a penchant for really rich chocolate, this is the cake for you. It only rises a little in baking and tends to drop when cold, but then it develops the most deliciously fudgy texture. It is very good covered with whipped cream, or rich chocolate icing (see page 147), which makes it into a most sumptuous dessert.

INGREDIENTS
For the cake
160g (5½ oz) plain chocolate

30g (1oz) unsalted butter

1 egg yolk

60g (2oz) caster sugar, sifted

4 egg whites

For the decoration
150ml (¼ pint) double cream

60g (2oz) plain chocolate, finely grated

1 For the cake, melt the chocolate and butter (see page 44) and leave to cool.

2 Whisk the egg yolk and 1 tablespoon of the sugar together until pale and fluffy. Stir in the melted chocolate.

3 In another bowl, whisk the egg whites into soft peaks. Gradually whisk in the rest of the sugar until they form stiff, glossy peaks (see page 49). Carefully stir 2 large spoonfuls into the main mixture to loosen the texture, then gently fold in the remainder until everything is evenly mixed.

4 Pour the mixture into the prepared tin and bake in the preheated oven for about 30–35 minutes or until a skewer inserted into the cake comes out clean. Remove from the oven and leave to rest in the tin for 10 minutes. Take out of the tin and leave to cool on a wire rack.

5 Carefully peel off the lining paper and transfer the cake to a serving plate. Whip the cream into stiff peaks. Spread evenly over the top of the cake and sprinkle with the grated chocolate to decorate.

 Oven temperature
180°C/350°F/gas 4

 Baking time
30–35 minutes

 Cake tin
18cm (7in) springform tin, greased and base-lined

 Makes
8 slices

 Storage
Keeps for 3–4 days

Freezing
Freezes for 1–2 months, undecorated

Caracas

This stylish, elegantly shaped chocolate log is baked in a Balmoral tin and covered with a thick layer of chocolate ganache. It is excellent served with a cup of dark coffee. (See page 14 for illustration.)

INGREDIENTS
For the cake
30g (1oz) plain chocolate

1 tbsp cold water

3 eggs, separated

30g (1oz) icing sugar, sifted

45g (1½ oz) ground almonds

1 tbsp caster sugar

1½ tbsp plain flour, sifted

25g (¾ oz) butter, melted and cooled

For the filling and decoration
175ml (6fl oz) double cream

200g (7oz) plain chocolate, grated

10 square chocolate thins, halved

1 For the cake, melt the chocolate with the water (see page 44) and leave to cool. Whisk the egg yolks and icing sugar to the ribbon stage (see page 48). Stir in the chocolate and almonds.

2 In another bowl, whisk the egg whites into soft peaks. Whisk in the caster sugar. Stir 2 large spoonfuls into the main mixture to loosen the texture. Gently fold in the flour and melted butter, followed by the remaining egg whites.

3 Pour the mixture into the prepared tin and bake in the preheated oven for 25 minutes or until a skewer inserted into the cake comes out clean. Remove from the oven, turn out on to a wire rack and leave to cool.

4 Cut a right-angled wedge lengthways out of the top of the cake. Make the filling as for chocolate ganache (see page 151). Spoon one quarter into a piping bag fitted with a 1cm (½in) star nozzle. Spread a little ganache into the cavity and replace the wedge. Spread the remainder over the cake and mark with horizontal lines using a knife. Pipe ganache down the centre in 10 swirls and decorate with the halved chocolate thins.

 Oven temperature
180°C/350°F/gas 4

 Baking time
25 minutes

 Cake tin
27x11cm (10½ x 4½ in) Balmoral tin, greased and floured

 Makes
10 slices

 Storage
Keeps for 1 week

 Freezing
Freezes for 1 month

Poppy Seed & Chocolate Torte

Intensely moist in texture, this Hungarian cake from the 19th century includes poppy seeds, which give an unusual flavour, handsomely complemented by raisins and dark chocolate. Serve with whipped cream on the side.

INGREDIENTS

For the cake

90g (3oz) raisins

2 tbsp boiling water

90g (3oz) plain chocolate

125g (4oz) butter

125g (4oz) caster sugar

1 tsp finely grated lemon zest

6 eggs, separated

2 tbsp toasted breadcrumbs, finely ground (see page 45)

150g (5oz) poppy seeds, finely ground (see Poppy Seed Strudel page 104)

For the filling and decoration

75ml (5 tbsp) black cherry jam, sieved and warmed

1 quantity of rich chocolate icing (see page 147)

4–6 quantities chocolate caraque (see page 146)

icing sugar

1 Soak the raisins in the water for 30 minutes. Drain and pat dry. Melt the chocolate (see page 44) and leave to cool.

2 Beat the butter, sugar and lemon zest together until pale and fluffy. Beat in the egg yolks, one at a time, then the chocolate, breadcrumbs and raisins.

3 In another bowl, whisk the egg whites into soft peaks. Stir 2 large spoonfuls into the main mixture to loosen the texture. Gently fold in the poppy seeds and the remaining egg whites until evenly mixed.

4 Pour the mixture carefully into the prepared tin and bake in the preheated oven for 45 minutes or until a skewer inserted into the cake comes out clean. Turn out on to a wire rack, peel off the lining paper and leave to cool.

5 Slice the cake horizontally in half and sandwich together with 2 tablespoons of the jam. Spread the remaining jam over the top and sides of the cake. Pour on the rich chocolate icing and tilt to cover (see page 147). Cover the top with the chocolate caraque to decorate and leave to set. Dust with icing sugar just before serving.

  Oven temperature
160°C/325°F/gas 3

 Baking time
45 minutes

 Cake tin
22cm (8½in) springform tin, greased and base-lined

 Makes
16–20 slices

 Storage
Keeps for 4–5 days

 Freezing
Freezes for 1–2 months, undecorated

Step ahead
Soak the raisins; prepare the toasted breadcrumbs and the poppy seeds; make the chocolate caraque

Fresh Fruit Cakes

There is something magical about fruit that hangs heavy, ripening on the tree bough in a trellis of green foliage. It has inspired us to write and to paint, and of course to cook and bake. The lavish and abundant harvests in the fruit-growing areas of the world have encouraged cooks to develop many regional specialities, and the resulting combinations of fresh, luscious, brightly coloured fruit in cakes and batters have a delicious, mouthwatering appeal that never fails to please the eye and delight the palate.

FRESH PLUM GENOESE, a moist but light and buttery sponge baked between two layers of sliced juicy red plums.

Fresh Plum Genoese

The natural juiciness and tartness of plums make this cake moist, but not too sweet. My favourite plums for cooking are the dark red Switzen, which appear only in mid-autumn. They are richly flavoured and hold their shape well without becoming too watery during baking. Small, golden-yellow French Mirabelle plums and greengages are very successful too.

INGREDIENTS

625g (1¼ lb) plums

For the cake

60g (2oz) butter, melted and cooled

125g (4oz) caster sugar

4 large eggs (size 1), separated

1 tsp finely grated lemon zest

125g (4oz) plain flour, sifted

caster sugar to decorate

1 Wash and dry the plums. Cut in half, remove the stones and slice the flesh thickly. Arrange half the slices over the base of the prepared tin.

2 Make the cake mixture following the method for Rich Genoese Sponge (see page 67). Pour over the plums and bake in the preheated oven for 15 minutes or until just set.

3 Open the oven door, pull out the shelf, leaving the tin on it, and arrange the remaining plum slices neatly over the top in concentric circles. Slide the shelf back in and cook for a further 30–35 minutes or until a skewer inserted into the cake comes out clean.

4 Remove from the oven and leave to cool in the tin. Take the cake out of the tin, peel off the lining paper and transfer to a serving plate. Dust with a little caster sugar to decorate. Serve slightly warm or cold with cream if you wish.

VARIATION
This sponge can also be made using peeled and cored dessert apples, cut into 5mm (¼in) thick slices.

 Oven temperature
180°C/350°F/gas 4

 Baking time
45–50 minutes

 Cake tin
20cm (8in) springform tin, greased, base-lined, greased once more and then dusted with flour and sugar

 Makes
8 slices

 Storage
Keeps for 2–3 days in the refrigerator

 Freezing
Freezes for 1–2 months

Italian Pear & Nut Sponge

INGREDIENTS

750g (1½ lb) firm, ripe pears

2 tbsp lemon juice

225g (7½ oz) plain flour

pinch of salt

1½ tsp bicarbonate of soda

1 tsp ground ginger

125ml (4fl oz) sunflower oil

165g (5½ oz) caster sugar

1 egg

1 egg yolk

1 tsp finely grated lemon zest

60g (2oz) walnuts, coarsely chopped

100g (3½ oz) sultanas

icing sugar to decorate

1 Peel and core the pears and cut into small chunks. Sprinkle with the lemon juice to prevent discoloration. Sift the flour, salt, bicarbonate of soda and ginger together. Set aside with the pears.

2 Put the oil, caster sugar, whole egg and egg yolk into

a bowl and beat together well. Gradually stir in the flour, a spoonful at a time, taking care not to overbeat the mixture.

3 Stir the lemon zest, chopped walnuts and sultanas into the mixture, followed by the pear pieces, making sure that everything is evenly mixed.

4 Pour the mixture into the prepared tin and bake in the preheated oven for about 1 hour 10 minutes or until golden and a skewer inserted into the cake comes out clean. (It may need a little longer cooking, depending on the ripeness of the pears.)

5 Remove the cake from the oven and leave to rest in the tin for 10 minutes. Take the cake out of the tin, carefully peel off the lining paper and leave to cool on a wire rack. Transfer to a plate and dust with a little icing sugar to decorate. Serve with whipped cream.

 Oven temperature
180°C/350°F/gas 4

 Baking time
1 hour 10 minutes

 Cake tin
22cm (8½in) springform tin, greased and base-lined

 Makes
8 slices

 Storage
Keeps for 2–3 days

 Freezing
Freezes for 1–2 months

Swiss Black Cherry Cake

A popular cake in the orchard regions of Europe, this is a peasant recipe similar to a French "Clafoutis", a sweet, thick, fruit-laden pancake. The recipe includes ground almonds and breadcrumbs to give a richer flavour and enhance its keeping quality.

INGREDIENTS

90g (3oz) stale white bread
100ml (3½ fl oz) milk, warmed
90ml (6 tbsp) hot water
2 tbsp fresh white breadcrumbs
125g (4oz) caster sugar
3 eggs, separated
60g (2oz) butter, melted and cooled
75g (2½ oz) ground almonds
1 tsp ground cinnamon
750g (1½ lb) black or morello cherries, washed, dried and stoned
pinch of salt
icing sugar to decorate

1 Break the stale bread into small pieces. Put into a bowl, stir in the milk and water and set aside to soak for 15 minutes. Sprinkle the prepared cake tin with the fresh breadcrumbs.

2 Set aside 2 tablespoons of the caster sugar. Whisk the remainder with the egg yolks until smooth. Gradually whisk in the melted butter until the mixture is pale and creamy. Carefully stir in the ground almonds and cinnamon.

3 Drain the bread in a sieve and squeeze out any excess liquid by hand. Beat to a paste with a fork. Stir into the main mixture with the cherries.

4 In another bowl, whisk the egg whites and salt into soft peaks. Sift over the reserved sugar and whisk into slightly stiffer peaks (see page 49). Stir 2 large spoonfuls into the main mixture to loosen the texture, then gently fold in the remainder until evenly mixed.

5 Pour the mixture into the tin and bake in the preheated oven for 1–1¼ hours until golden. Remove from the oven and leave to rest for 10 minutes. Turn out on to a wire rack, peel off the lining paper and leave to cool. Dust with icing sugar to serve.

 Oven temperature
180°C/350°F/gas 4

 Baking time
1–1¼ hours

 Cake tin
22cm (8½ in) springform tin, greased and base-lined

 Makes
8–10 slices

 Storage
Keeps for 1–2 days

 Freezing
Freezes for 1–2 months

 Step ahead
Stone the cherries

Devonshire Apple Cake

This simple cake has a moist, pudding-like texture that appeals particularly to children. It comes from a booklet entitled Recipes, Remedies and Rhymes *(1976), which was produced by a group of villagers in Devon, England, to raise funds for their local church. Serve with whipped cream.*

INGREDIENTS

2 quantities apple purée (see page 149)
125g (4oz) butter, softened
2 eggs, separated
125g (4oz) fresh white breadcrumbs
2 tsp ground cinnamon
60g (2oz) currants
45g (1½ oz) cornflour, sifted
1 large dessert apple
1 tbsp granulated sugar

1 Make the apple purée and set aside to cool. Beat the butter and egg yolks together until thick and creamy. Stir in the apple purée, breadcrumbs, half the cinnamon and currants. Sift over the cornflour and fold in.

2 In another bowl, whisk the egg whites into soft peaks. Stir 2 large spoonfuls into the main mixture to loosen the texture, then gently fold in the remainder until everything is evenly mixed.

3 Pour the mixture carefully into the prepared tin. Peel, core and thinly slice the dessert apple. Arrange around the top edge of the cake.

4 Bake in the preheated oven for 1 hour 10 minutes or until a skewer inserted into the cake comes out clean.

5 Remove from the oven and leave to cool on a wire rack. Take out of the tin and peel off the lining paper. Transfer to a serving plate and sprinkle with the granulated sugar and the remaining cinnamon to decorate.

 Oven temperature
180°C/350°F/gas 4

 Baking time
1 hour 10 minutes

 Cake tin
22cm (8½ in) springform tin, greased, base-lined and dusted with sugar and flour

 Makes
8 slices

 Storage
Keeps for 2–3 days

 Freezing
Freezes for 1–2 months

Step ahead
Make the apple purée

American Carrot Loaf

A few years ago I suggested this tea loaf as an entry for our annual village flower and produce show. The first year I baked one myself and persuaded a friend to do the same. Ours were the only entries! The following year there were a few more attempts and it is now a regular feature. Bake it 2–3 days ahead of time to allow the flavours to mature before decorating. (See page 23 for illustration.)

INGREDIENTS

For the cake

180g (6oz) plain flour

1½ tsp baking powder

½ tsp bicarbonate of soda

pinch of salt

1 tsp ground cinnamon

180g (6oz) carrots, peeled and grated

90g (3oz) roasted hazelnuts, chopped

150g (5oz) light muscovado sugar

2 eggs

finely grated zest of 1 orange

75g (2½ oz) butter, melted and cooled

For the decoration

1 quantity cream cheese frosting (see page 150)

16 marzipan carrots (see page 148)

15g (½ oz) roasted hazelnuts, chopped

coarse strands of orange zest (see page 149)

1 For the cake, sift the flour, baking powder, bicarbonate of soda, salt and cinnamon together. Pat the carrot dry and mix in a bowl with the nuts and sugar. Beat in the eggs, one at a time, followed by the zest and butter. Gently fold in the flour.

2 Pour the mixture into the prepared tin and bake in the preheated oven for 50 minutes–1 hour or until a skewer inserted into the cake comes out clean. Remove from the oven and leave to rest for 10 minutes. Turn out on to a wire rack, peel off the lining paper and leave to cool.

3 Spread the frosting over the top of the cake using a palette knife, and decorate with the marzipan carrots, hazelnuts and strands of orange zest.

 Oven temperature
180°C/350°F/gas 4

 Baking time
50 minutes–1 hour

 Cake tin
1kg (2lb) loaf tin, greased and lined

 Makes
12 slices

 Storage
Keeps for 4–6 days

 Freezing
Freezes for 1–2 months, undecorated

Pecan & Banana Layer Cake

Americans from the Southern States have a weak spot for all things banana – and this rich banana and lime cream filling, taken from Mrs Dull's Georgia cookery book, Southern Cooking *(1928), turns the simple banana loaf into a more exciting cake that children seem to adore.*

INGREDIENTS

For the cake

125g (4oz) butter

250g (8oz) muscovado sugar

2 large ripe bananas, peeled and mashed

2 eggs, lightly beaten

1 tsp finely grated lime zest

1 tbsp bicarbonate of soda

2 tbsp boiling water

125g (4oz) pecan nuts, coarsely chopped

250g (8oz) plain flour, sifted

For the filling

4 medium bananas, peeled and mashed

3 tbsp lime juice

4 tbsp caster sugar

3 tbsp cornflour, sifted

For the decoration

90ml (3fl oz) double cream, whipped

125g (4oz) pecan nuts, finely chopped

1 For the cake, beat the butter and sugar together until pale and fluffy. Gradually beat in the bananas, eggs and lime zest. Dissolve the bicarbonate of soda in the water and gently stir in. Carefully mix in the pecan nuts and the flour.

2 Pour the mixture into the prepared tin and bake in the preheated oven for 1 hour or until a skewer inserted into the cake comes out clean. Remove from the oven and leave to rest for 10 minutes. Turn out on to a wire rack, peel off the lining paper and leave to cool.

3 For the filling, push the bananas through a sieve into a heatproof bowl. Stir in the lime juice, sugar and cornflour. Rest the bowl over a pan of simmering water and cook, stirring, for 10 minutes or until thick. Leave to cool.

4 Slice the cake horizontally into three layers. Sandwich together with the filling. Spread the whipped cream over the top of the cake and sprinkle with the pecan nuts to decorate.

 Oven temperature
180°C/350°F/gas 4

 Baking time
1 hour

 Cake tin
1kg (2lb) loaf tin, greased and base-lined

Makes
8–10 slices

Storage
Leave to mature for 1 day before serving; keeps for 3–4 days

 Freezing
Freezes for 1–2 months, undecorated

Flans & Tarts

A 13th-century Arab manuscript describes a tart filled with a syrupy nut, date and poppy seed mixture, flavoured with rose water, tinted with saffron, and cooked with a roasting chicken suspended above, dripping juices on to the tart. Today flans and tarts excite in a more familiar way. Crisp pastry encases jewel-like berries or citrus slices. Caramelized fruit juices and vanilla creams enhance the flavour and nuts give texture.

French Flan with Red Berries

Rings of colourful, fresh summer berries over a rich and creamy filling within a sweet pastry case look attractive and tempting.

Making the Flan

Flavour the crème pâtissière with fresh vanilla if you can. It has a much more subtle and delicate flavour than vanilla extract and the pod can be rinsed off, allowed to dry and saved for another occasion.

INGREDIENTS

For the flan case

1 quantity pâte sablée pastry (see page 55)

For the filling

2 tbsp apricot jam, sieved

1 quantity crème pâtissière (see page 151)

750g (1½ lb) strawberries, raspberries and blueberries or other soft fruit

For the decoration

1 quantity redcurrant glaze (see page 149)

icing sugar

1 Allow the pastry to come back to room temperature. Knead briefly until smooth, roll out on a lightly floured surface and use to line the prepared tin (see page 56). Chill for 1 hour.

2 Prick the base all over with a fork and bake blind (see page 56) in the preheated oven for 10 minutes. Remove the paper and beans or foil and bake for a further 10–15 minutes or until it is crisp and golden. Remove from the oven and leave to cool on a wire rack.

3 Brush the base of the pastry case with the apricot jam. Spoon in the crème pâtissière and spread evenly over the base with a small palette knife or the back of a spoon. Arrange the prepared fruit close together in concentric circles over the top of the crème pâtissière.

4 Spoon the redcurrant glaze evenly over the fruit up to the edge of the pastry so that it forms a seal, and leave to set. Remove from the tin, transfer to a serving plate and dust the edges of the pastry lightly with icing sugar just before serving.

  Oven temperature
200°C/400°F/gas 6

 Baking time
20–25 minutes

 Flan tin
23cm (9in) fluted flan tin, greased

 Makes
8 slices

Storage
Keeps for 1–2 days

 Step ahead
Make the crème pâtissière; make the pastry and chill for 1 hour; make the redcurrant glaze

Special Ingredients

Mixed berries such as blueberries, raspberries and strawberries are deliciously sweet yet tart in flavour. They taste best when picked fully ripe. Wash them briefly with their stalks intact to retain errant juices, then dry on kitchen paper. They should not be sugared.

Blueberries

Raspberries

Vanilla pods give the crème pâtissière its wonderful flavour.

Strawberries

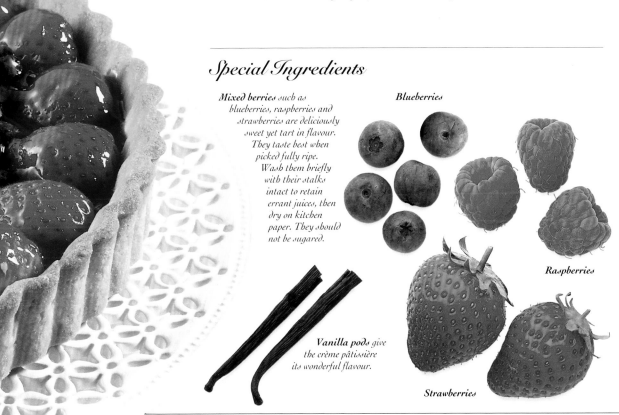

Glazed Fresh Orange Flan

This is an unusual and colourful flan filled with freshly glazed oranges. Be sure to score the skin of the oranges thoroughly before simmering the slices in the syrup otherwise they become tough and chewy. (See page 19 for illustration.)

INGREDIENTS

For the flan case

1 quantity pâte sablée pastry (see page 55)

For the filling and decoration

3 tbsp icing sugar, sifted

1 quantity orange mousseline buttercream (see page 150)

375g (12oz) granulated sugar

125ml (4fl oz) fresh orange juice, strained

125ml (4fl oz) fresh lemon juice, strained

5 unwaxed, small, thin-skinned oranges

1 tbsp dark rum or 1 tsp orange-flower water

1 Allow the pastry to come back to room temperature. Knead briefly until smooth, roll out and use to line the prepared tin (see page 56). Prick the base all over with a fork and chill for 1 hour. Bake blind (see page 56) in the preheated oven for 10 minutes. Uncover and bake for a further 10–15 minutes. Remove from the oven and leave to cool.

2 For the filling, beat the icing sugar into the buttercream, then spread it over the base of the pastry case. Chill for 1 hour.

3 Put the sugar, orange juice and lemon juice into a large, deep frying pan. Leave over a low heat until the sugar has dissolved. Bring to the boil and simmer for 20 minutes.

4 Score the skin of the oranges from the stalk end to the navel with a cannelling or small sharp knife. Cut across into 2.5mm (⅛in) thick slices. Lower into the syrup and simmer for 20–30 minutes or until tender. Lift the slices on to a wire rack and leave to drain for 1 hour.

5 Boil the syrup until reduced and thickened. Stir in the rum or flower water and leave to cool. Arrange the orange slices over the buttercream and spoon over a thin layer of syrup. Remove from the tin to serve.

 Oven temperature
200°C/400°F/gas 6

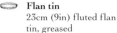 **Baking time**
20–25 minutes for the flan case

 Flan tin
23cm (9in) fluted flan tin, greased

 Makes
8–10 slices

 Storage
Keeps for 1 week

 Step ahead
Make the pastry and chill for 1 hour; make the orange mousseline buttercream

Fresh Fig Flan

One summer some years ago we stayed with friends on their farm in Tuscany, Italy. The neighbours were away and had asked us to tend their garden, and as a reward we could help ourselves to its produce. The fig trees were laden with luscious, purple fruit that simply had to be eaten. This delicious flan reminds me of that hot, golden summer.

INGREDIENTS

For the flan case

1 quantity pâte sablée pastry (see page 55)

For the filling

60g (2oz) ground almonds

60g (2oz) icing sugar

60g (2oz) unsalted butter, softened

1 egg

1 tsp finely grated lemon zest

375g (12oz) fresh figs, halved

3 tbsp simple sugar syrup (see page 155)

1 tbsp fresh lemon juice, strained

icing sugar to decorate

1 Allow the pastry to come back to room temperature. Knead briefly until smooth, roll out and use to line the prepared tin (see page 56). Prick the base all over with a fork and chill for 1 hour. Bake blind (see page 56) in the preheated oven for 10 minutes. Uncover and bake for a further 10 minutes. Remove from the oven and leave to cool. Reduce the oven temperature.

2 For the filling, beat together the almonds, sugar, butter, egg and lemon zest until smooth. Spread evenly over the bottom of the pastry case. Lay the figs, cut side up, on top of the filling.

3 Mix the sugar syrup with the lemon juice. Spoon over the figs and bake for 45 minutes. Remove from the oven and leave to cool on a wire rack. Take out of the tin and dust with icing sugar to decorate.

 Oven temperature
200°C/400°F/gas 6, for the flan case; 190°C/375°F/gas 5 for the filling

 Baking time
20 minutes for the flan case; 45 minutes for the filling

 Flan tin
23cm (9in) fluted flan tin, greased

 Makes
8–10 slices

 Storage
Best eaten the day it is made

Step ahead
Make the pastry and chill for 1 hour; make the simple sugar syrup

Pecan & Maple Pie

A great American classic from my good friend Nancy Greer, this is her "pièce de résistance" at dinner parties. Pecans grow on hickory trees and the cultivated varieties were developed in Louisiana sugar country. The shelled nuts look a little like walnuts but are more crisp and oily, and the flavour is milder. Pecans and maple syrup blended in a pie make an irresistible combination.

INGREDIENTS

For the flan case

1 quantity pâte brisée pastry (see page 54)

For the filling

90g (3oz) butter

125g (4oz) light muscovado sugar

3 eggs

100ml (3½fl oz) maple syrup

150ml (¼ pint) golden syrup

1 tbsp Kentucky bourbon or dark rum

pinch of salt

150g (5oz) pecan nuts, coarsely chopped

1 tbsp plain flour

250g (8oz) pecan halves to decorate

1 Allow the pastry to come back to room temperature. Knead briefly until smooth, roll out on a lightly floured surface and use to line the prepared tin (see page 56). Chill for 1 hour. Bake blind (see page 56) in the preheated oven for 20 minutes. Remove from the oven, uncover and lower the oven temperature.

2 For the filling, beat the butter and sugar together until pale and fluffy. Beat in the eggs, one at a time. Slowly mix in the maple syrup and golden syrup, followed by the bourbon or dark rum and salt.

3 Mix the chopped pecan nuts with the flour and then carefully fold them into the main mixture. Pour into the flan case and bake in the preheated oven for 15 minutes until the filling is lightly set.

4 Remove the pie from the oven and arrange the pecan halves in concentric circles over the top of the partially set filling. Return to the oven and bake for another 30–40 minutes or until completely set; cover with domed foil halfway through if it starts to over-brown. Remove from the oven and leave to cool on a wire rack. Take out of the tin and serve warm or cold with cream.

Oven temperature
200°C/400°F/gas 6 for the flan case; 180°C/350°F/gas 4 for the filling

Baking time
20 minutes for the flan case; 45–55 minutes for the filling

Flan tin
22cm (8½in), 3.5cm (1½in) deep, fluted flan tin, greased

Makes
8–10 slices

Storage
Keeps for 3–4 days

Step ahead
Make the pastry and chill for 1 hour

Linzertorte

This is a rather special, festive jam tart with a distinctive lattice top. It has 18th-century Teutonic origins and remains very popular in America and throughout Europe. Traditionally, it is made with ground almonds but modern-day variations often use hazelnuts. Mature for at least one week before serving.

INGREDIENTS

For the pastry

200g (7oz) plain flour

½ tsp ground cinnamon

pinch of ground cloves

200g (7oz) chilled butter, cut into pieces

150g (5oz) roasted hazelnuts, finely ground (see page 45)

100g (3½ oz) toasted breadcrumbs, finely ground (see page 45)

200g (7oz) caster sugar

1 egg, lightly beaten

1–2 tbsp dark rum

For the filling and decoration

250g (8oz) raspberry or redcurrant jam, sieved

2 tbsp milk

1 egg yolk, lightly beaten

1 For the pastry, sift the flour and spices together. Add the butter and rub together into a fine crumb-like mixture. Stir in the hazelnuts, breadcrumbs and sugar, followed by the egg and rum until the mixture starts to stick together. Knead briefly until smooth. Cut off one third, wrap each piece in clingfilm, and chill for 1 hour.

2 Allow the pastry to come back to room temperature. Roll out the larger piece between silicone paper to a thickness of 5mm (¼in). Use to line the prepared tin (see page 56). Prick all over with a fork and spread with two thirds of the jam.

3 Roll out the remaining pastry and cut into 1cm (½in) wide strips. Arrange over the tart in a lattice design (see page 133), sealing to the edge with milk.

4 Brush with the egg yolk and bake in the preheated oven for 30 minutes. Remove from the oven, spoon the remaining jam into each space between the pastry lattice and leave to cool. Remove from the tin to serve.

 Oven temperature
200°C/400°F/gas 6

 Baking time
30 minutes

 Flan tin
23cm (9in) fluted flan tin, greased

 Makes
8–10 slices

 Storage
Leave to mature for at least 1 week before serving; keeps for 4–5 weeks

 Step ahead
Make the pastry and chill for 1 hour

Fresh Plum Pastry

An unusual sweet and soft German pastry forms the base for my mother's plum cake. The pastry rises between the fruit as it cooks and the slightly tart juices ooze deliciously into the mixture. It can also be made with nectarines, apricots, apples and other fruit that holds its shape.

INGREDIENTS

For the German pastry

125g (4oz) self-raising flour

125g (4oz) chilled butter, cut into pieces

75g (2½ oz) caster sugar

1 tsp finely grated lemon zest

1 egg yolk

For the topping

625g (1¼ lb) fresh plums (Switzen if possible)

1 tsp ground cinnamon

1–2 tbsp caster sugar to decorate

1 For the pastry, sift the flour into a bowl, add the butter and rub together into a fine crumb-like mixture. Mix in the sugar and zest. Stir in the egg yolk until everything starts to stick together. Knead briefly on a surface lightly dusted with flour until smooth. Wrap in clingfilm and chill for 1 hour.

2 Allow the pastry to come back to room temperature. Knead briefly once more until smooth, then lightly press on to the base of the prepared tin.

3 Wash and dry the plums, cut in half and remove the stones. Tightly pack the fruit, skin-side down, on to the pastry base but do not press them in. Sprinkle over the cinnamon and bake in the preheated oven for 50 minutes–1 hour or until the pastry is golden and the fruit is cooked through.

4 Remove the pastry from the oven and leave to rest for 5 minutes. Sprinkle the top with the caster sugar and leave to cool on a wire rack. Cut into slices and remove from the tin. Serve with a little whipped cream if you wish.

 Oven temperature
190°C/375°F/gas 5

 Baking time
50 minutes–1 hour

 Cake tin
30x18x1.5cm (12x7x¾ in) shallow, rectangular tin, or a 22cm (8½ in) springform tin, greased

 Makes
8 slices

 Storage
Keeps for 2–3 days

 Freezing
Freezes for 1–2 months

 Step ahead
Make the pastry and chill for 1 hour

Tarte Tatin

Who can resist succulent, buttery, caramel-flavoured fruit resting on the simplest of shortcrust pastry crusts? The pastry sits on top of the apples during cooking so that when the tart is turned over, the caramelized juices dribble down over the base. It is traditional to make this in a moule à manquer *tin*, which has a fixed base and sloping sides, so that none of the juices are lost during the cooking process. (See page 18 for illustration.)

INGREDIENTS

For the pastry

1 quantity pâte brisée pastry (see page 54)

For the topping

1.5kg (3lb) small dessert apples

90g (3oz) butter

100g (3½ oz) granulated sugar

1 Allow the pastry to come back to room temperature. Remove the cores from the apples with an apple corer. Peel and cut them in half.

2 For the topping, put the butter and sugar into a large saucepan or deep frying pan. Heat gently until melted. Cook, stirring now and then, until the mixture starts to caramelize and turn a light brown.

3 Take the pan off the heat and add the apple halves. Gently turn them over in the mixture until well coated, return to a high heat and cook, stirring gently now and then, for 10 minutes or until the sauce has

thickened even more and the apples are golden brown.

4 Pack the apples tightly into the bottom of the tin, rounded-side down. Roll out the pastry on a lightly floured surface into a circle slightly larger than the top of the tin. Lift carefully on to the apples and tuck the edges down well around the fruit.

5 Bake in the preheated oven for 20 minutes or until the pastry is golden brown.

6 Remove from the oven and leave to rest in the tin for 5 minutes so that the juices have time to set slightly; but do not leave longer or the caramel sauce and the apples will stick to the base of the tin and not to the tart.

7 Run a round-bladed knife around the edge of the pastry and carefully turn out the tart on to a plate. Leave to cool slightly. Serve warm with whipped cream.

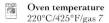

Oven temperature
220°C/425°F/gas 7

Baking time
20 minutes

Cake tin
24cm (9½ in) moule à manquer tin or heavy-based, shallow, round cake tin

Makes
8 slices

Storage
Best eaten as soon as it is made

Step ahead
Make the pastry and chill for 1 hour

Tarte au Citron

If you are fond of citrus fruit then this is an especially fine tart to make. The rich and creamy filling with its sharp lemon tang is complemented by fine-textured, light, crispy pastry. Variations of this French classic are to be found in every chef pâtissier's repertoire. It tastes its very best when still slightly warm from the oven.

INGREDIENTS

For the flan case

1 quantity pâte sablée pastry (see page 55)

For the filling

3 eggs

125g (4oz) caster sugar

2 tsp finely grated lemon zest

juice of 2 lemons

100ml (3½ fl oz) double cream

icing sugar to decorate

1 Allow the pastry to come back to room temperature. Knead briefly until smooth, roll out and use to line the prepared tin (see page 56). Prick the base all over with a fork and chill for 1 hour. Bake blind (see page 56) in the preheated oven for

10 minutes. Uncover and return to the oven for a further 10–15 minutes.

2 For the filling, mix the eggs and sugar together lightly until pale and creamy but not frothy. Stir in the lemon zest and juice. Fold in the cream and skim off any bubbles.

3 Remove the flan case from the oven and lower the oven temperature. Pour the filling straight into the hot case; this helps it to set and make a seal. Return to the oven and bake for 30 minutes or until set. Remove from the oven and leave to cool on a wire rack. Take out of the tin and dust with icing sugar just before serving.

Oven temperature
200°C/400°F/gas 6 for the flan case;
120°C/250°F/gas ½ for the filling

Baking time
20–25 minutes for the flan case;
30 minutes for the filling

Flan tin
Shallow 23cm (9in) fluted flan tin, greased

Makes
8 slices

Storage
Best eaten as soon as it is made

Fruit & Spice Cakes

Figs, dates and grapes, ripened in the sun and dried in hot sand, were a staple in the early Middle Eastern diet and eventually spread worldwide. Spices were imported from the Orient and so highly valued that demand for them caused centuries of warfare. In Arabia, fruit and spices were wrapped in pastry, and in northern Europe they were kneaded into bread doughs. In time, eggs, sugar, butter and alcohol were introduced to the mixture to create rich fruit cakes.

THE CAKE IS MOIST *and rich in flavour, packed full of apricots, sultanas, glacé cherries and pineapple.*

Brandied Fruit Cake

Special Ingredients

Pecan nuts *give an attractive crunch to the cake's topping.*

Dried apricots and sultanas *are softened by boiling with sugar and butter. This also intensifies their flavour.*

Glacé fruit *adds good colour and flavour to both the cake mixture and the decorative topping.*

Lemon zest *is the sharply aromatic outer layer of the fruit's skin.*

Brandy *adds a distinctive mellow warmth to the flavour of the cake.*

Marmalade *gives the cake a sharp, fruity tang to counteract the sweet glacé fruit.*

Making the Cake

Give a more festive alcoholic kick to this easy cake before decorating, with a weekly feed of two tablespoons of brandy, for two to three weeks (see step 5 in the Traditional English Plumb Cake, page 99).

INGREDIENTS

For the cake

375g (12oz) strong plain flour

1 tbsp baking powder

400ml (14fl oz) water

180g (6oz) butter, cut into pieces

375g (12oz) caster sugar

180g (6oz) dried apricots, quartered

375g (12oz) sultanas

125g (4oz) glacé cherries, washed, dried and halved

60g (2oz) glacé pineapple, diced

90ml (6 tbsp) brandy

3 eggs, lightly beaten

finely grated zest of 1 orange

finely grated zest of 1 lemon

For the decoration

4 tbsp shredless orange marmalade

60g (2oz) natural glacé cherries, halved

60g (2oz) red glacé cherries, halved

125g (4oz) glacé or crystallized pineapple pieces, halved if thick

125g (4oz) pecan nuts

60g (2oz) angelica, washed, dried and cut into diamonds

1 For the cake, sift the flour and baking powder together twice. Set aside. Put the water, butter, sugar, apricots and sultanas into a pan. Slowly bring to the boil over a low heat, then boil gently for 20 minutes, stirring now and then. Leave to cool.

2 Pour the boiled fruit mixture into a large bowl and stir in the glacé cherries, glacé pineapple and brandy. Beat in the eggs, followed by the orange and lemon zest. Add the flour and beat together until everything is evenly mixed.

3 Pour the mixture into the prepared tin and level the surface. Bake in the preheated oven for 2 hours or until a skewer inserted into the cake comes out clean. Cover with domed foil during baking if the top starts to over-brown.

4 Remove from the oven and leave in the tin on a wire rack to cool. Turn out of the tin once cold and carefully peel off the lining paper.

5 For the decoration, put the marmalade into a small pan and warm over a gentle heat. Brush half over the top of the cake and arrange the glacé fruit, nuts and angelica in diagonal lines across the top of the cake. Brush with the remaining marmalade to glaze. Leave to cool before serving.

 Oven temperature 160°C/325°F/gas 3

 Baking time 2 hours

 Cake tin 20cm (8in) deep, square tin, greased and double-lined with silicone paper

 Makes 24 slices

 Storage Keeps for 1–2 weeks

 Freezing Freezes for 3 months

Simple Ginger Cake

A cut-and-come-again cake from the north-east of England. It has a strong spicy flavour and the slow cooking produces a moist, sticky texture. Be sure that all the ingredients are at room temperature before you start, and then make it using an electric mixer.

INGREDIENTS

250g (8oz) self-raising flour
1 tsp ground ginger
125g (4oz) demerara sugar
175ml (6fl oz) golden syrup
2 eggs, lightly beaten
75ml (2½fl oz) sunflower or corn oil
125ml (4fl oz) warm water
90g (3oz) ginger marmalade or conserve

1 Sift the flour and ginger together into a bowl. Add the demerara sugar, golden syrup, eggs, oil, water and marmalade and beat together with an electric mixer until the mixture is pale and thick.

2 Pour the mixture into the prepared tin, place on a baking sheet and bake in the preheated oven for 2¼ hours or until a skewer inserted into the cake comes out clean.

3 Remove from the oven, turn out on to a wire rack and carefully peel off the lining paper. Leave to cool.

 Oven temperature
120°C/250°F/gas ½

 Baking time
2¼ hours

 Cake tin
1kg (2lb) loaf tin, greased and base-lined

 Makes
12–15 slices

Storage
Keeps for 5–6 days

Freezing
Freezes for 2 months

Spiced Honey Cake

Christmas honey cakes of northern Europe are usually spiced with cinnamon, ginger, cloves, aniseed and cardamom and can include almonds instead of rye flour. The mixture is traditionally left to stand for several days to mature and to allow natural leavening to occur. This is a lighter, less spicy cake which is enriched with eggs and soured cream.

INGREDIENTS

For the cake

165g (5½ oz) butter
325ml (11fl oz) honey
4 eggs, separated
165g (5½ oz) plain flour
1½ tsp ground cinnamon
1½ tsp ground ginger
1½ tsp ground cloves
1½ tsp baking powder
125g (4oz) rye flour
200ml (7fl oz) soured cream

For the decoration

1 quantity lemon glacé icing (see page 152)
thin slices of crystallized ginger

1 For the cake, melt the butter with the honey. Cool slightly, pour into a bowl and add the egg yolks. Beat together until pale, thick and frothy.

2 Sift together the plain flour, spices and baking powder. Stir in the rye flour. Fold into the egg yolk mixture, followed by the soured cream.

3 Whisk the egg whites into soft peaks. Gently fold into the egg yolk mixture. Pour into the prepared tin and bake in the preheated oven for 15 minutes. Lower the oven temperature and cook for 35–45 minutes.

4 Remove from the oven and leave for 5 minutes. Turn out on to a wire rack, peel off the lining paper and leave to cool. Spoon over the icing, decorate with the ginger and leave to set.

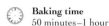 **Oven temperature**
160°C/325°F/gas 3, then
120°C/250°F/gas ½

 Baking time
50 minutes–1 hour

Cake tin
20cm (8in) square tin, greased and base-lined

Makes
9 large or 16 smaller squares

 Storage
Keeps for 1–2 weeks

Freezing
Freezes for 2–3 months, undecorated

Irish Barm Brack

Traditionally, this spiced bread was made with yeast and baked in a round pot over a peat fire. This is a quick and easy alternative. Serve in slices, spread with butter if you prefer.

INGREDIENTS

180g (6oz) currants

90g (3oz) sultanas

200ml (7fl oz) hot, black Darjeeling tea

90g (3oz) chopped mixed peel

250g (8oz) light soft brown sugar

½ tsp ground cinnamon

½ tsp ground allspice

2 eggs

2 tbsp fine-shred marmalade

1 tsp finely grated lemon zest

400g (13oz) self-raising flour, sifted

1 Put the currants and sultanas into a bowl and pour over the tea. Cover with clingfilm and soak overnight. The next day stir in the chopped mixed peel.

2 Put the sugar and spices into another bowl and beat in the eggs, one at a time. Stir in the marmalade and the lemon zest, followed by alternating spoonfuls of the tea and fruit mixture and the flour, until everything is evenly mixed.

3 Spoon the mixture into the prepared tin and level the surface. Bake in the preheated oven for 1–1¼ hours or until a skewer inserted into the cake comes out clean.

4 Remove the cake from the oven and leave in the tin on a wire rack to cool. Turn out of the tin once cold and peel off the lining paper.

 Oven temperature
180°C/350°F/gas 4

 Baking time
1–1¼ hours

 Cake tin
20cm (8in) deep, round tin, greased and base-lined

 Makes
12 slices

 Storage
Keeps for 1 week

 Freezing
Freezes for 1–2 months

Step ahead
Soak the dried fruit in the tea overnight

Traditional English Plumb Cake

For centuries now, the most costly and coveted cake ingredients – crystallized fruit, nuts and spices – have been made into a rich and dark cake served to mark festivals and celebrations. Lace it with spirits, cover it with marzipan, and finish with decorative icing for a traditional Christmas or wedding cake. (See page 27 for illustration.)

INGREDIENTS

125g (4oz) dried cranberries

125g (4oz) muscat raisins

180g (6oz) sultanas

180g (6oz) currants

180g (6oz) dried apricots, finely chopped

200ml (7fl oz) dark rum or brandy

1 tbsp finely grated orange zest

2 tbsp orange juice

300g (10oz) plain flour

1 tsp freshly grated nutmeg

1 tsp ground cinnamon

½ tsp ground allspice

125g (4oz) flaked almonds

250g (8oz) butter, softened

250g (8oz) light muscovado sugar

4 large eggs (size 1), lightly beaten

1 tbsp milk

60–90ml (4–6 tbsp) brandy for feeding

1 Put all the dried fruit, rum or brandy, orange zest and orange juice into a bowl. Mix well, cover with clingfilm and leave in a cool place for 24 hours.

2 The next day, sift the flour and spices together. Stir the flaked almonds and a little of the flour into the soaked fruit.

3 Beat the butter and sugar together until pale and fluffy. Gradually beat in the eggs. Stir in alternating spoonfuls of flour and dried fruit until everything is evenly mixed. Stir in the milk.

4 Spoon the mixture into the prepared tin, level the surface and make a slight dip in the centre. Put on to the prepared baking sheet and bake in the preheated oven for 2½ hours or until a skewer inserted into the cake comes out clean. Cover with a double sheet of greaseproof paper or foil halfway through to prevent over-browning.

5 Remove from the oven and leave in the tin on a wire rack to cool. Turn out and peel off the lining paper. Wrap in greaseproof paper and foil and store in an airtight tin. Once a week, for 2–3 weeks, pierce the bottom with a fine skewer, spoon over 2 tablespoons of extra brandy and rewrap.

 Oven temperature
150°C/300°F/gas 2

 Baking time
2½ hours

 Cake tins
20cm (8in) deep, round tin, greased and lined and protected with brown paper (see page 43); flat baking sheet, covered with a few layers of brown paper

 Makes
16 slices

 Storage
Keeps for 3 months

 Freezing
Freezes for 1 year

 Step ahead
Soak the dried fruit overnight

Chineser Brot

This is a fruited loaf taken from a 19th-century Austrian cookery book. I'm not sure why it is described as Chinese, but it may be because the dates and figs, with their fine, moist textures, hint at Far Eastern luxuries.

INGREDIENTS

For the cake

2 eggs, separated

1 egg yolk

60g (2oz) caster sugar

60g (2oz) unblanched almonds, coarsely ground

30g (1oz) plain chocolate, grated

1 tsp ground cinnamon

¼ tsp freshly grated nutmeg

25g (¾oz) dried figs, cut into slivers

25g (¾oz) sultanas

25g (¾oz) dried dates, cut into slivers

25g (¾oz) blanched almonds, sliced

25g (¾oz) toasted white breadcrumbs (see page 45)

For the decoration

½ quantity chocolate glacé icing (see page 152)

1 tbsp chopped blanched pistachio nuts

1 For the cake, whisk the egg yolks and sugar together to the ribbon stage (see page 48).

Mix the ground almonds, chocolate and spices together. Gently fold into the egg yolk mixture, followed by the dried fruit, almonds and breadcrumbs.

2 In another bowl, whisk the egg whites into soft peaks (see page 47). Stir 2 large spoonfuls into the main mixture to loosen the texture, then gently fold in the remainder.

3 Pour the mixture into the prepared tin and bake in the preheated oven for 25–30 minutes or until a skewer inserted into the cake comes out clean. Remove from the oven and leave to cool on a wire rack. Turn out and leave for two days.

TO FINISH THE CAKE
Place the cake flat-side down, on a wire rack. Pour over the icing (see page 142), sprinkle with the nuts and leave to set.

Oven temperature
180°C/350°F/gas 4

Baking time
25–30 minutes

Cake tin
27x11cm (10½ x 4½in) Balmoral tin, greased and floured

Makes .
14 slices

Storage
Leave to mature for 2 days before icing; keeps for 2 days once decorated

Freezing
Freezes for 1–2 months, undecorated

Bischofs Brot

In 19th-century northern Europe, a mulled red wine spiced with citrus peel, cinnamon and cloves, and known as a "Bischof", was often served at dances. The fine, spiced, nutty flavour of this loaf complements the drink very well.

INGREDIENTS

3 eggs, separated

150g (5oz) caster sugar

75g (2½oz) raisins

25g (¾oz) pine nuts, coarsely chopped

30g (1oz) pistachio nuts, coarsely chopped

45g (1½oz) blanched almonds, cut into slivers

1 tsp finely grated lemon zest

1 tsp ground cinnamon

½ tsp mixed spice

100g (3½oz) plain flour

2 tbsp flaked almonds

1 Whisk the egg yolks and sugar together to the ribbon stage (see page 48). Stir in the raisins, chopped pine nuts and pistachio nuts, slivered almonds and the lemon zest.

2 Sift the cinnamon, mixed spice and flour together. Stir

into the egg yolk mixture until evenly mixed.

3 In another bowl, whisk the egg whites into soft peaks (see page 47). Stir 2 large spoonfuls into the main mixture to loosen the texture, then gently fold in the remainder.

4 Spoon the mixture into the prepared tin and lightly level the surface. Sprinkle with the flaked almonds. Bake in the centre of the preheated oven for 50 minutes or until a skewer inserted into the middle of the cake comes out clean.

5 Remove the cake from the oven and leave in the tin on a wire rack to cool. Turn out and peel off the lining paper. Leave the cake for two days to allow the flavours to mature before serving.

Oven temperature
160°C/325°F/gas 3

Baking time
50 minutes

Cake tin
1kg (2lb) loaf tin, greased and base-lined

Makes
15 slices

Storage
Leave to mature for 2 days before serving; keeps for 1 week

Apricot & Pecan Tea Loaf

With a light, nutty crunch and a distinctive orange tang, this apricot-filled loaf is delicious served just as it is.

INGREDIENTS

For the cake

200g (7oz) dried apricots

75g (2½ oz) pecan nuts, chopped

250g (8oz) plain flour

¼ tsp salt

½ tsp bicarbonate of soda

100ml (3½ fl oz) milk

100g (3½ oz) butter

200g (7oz) caster sugar

2 large eggs (size 1), lightly beaten

finely grated zest of 1 large orange

½ tsp orange-flower water

For the syrup

2 tbsp orange juice

2 tbsp granulated sugar

pecan nuts and coarse strands of orange zest (see page 149) to decorate

1 Cover the apricots with cold water and soak overnight.

2 Drain, dry and chop the apricots. Mix with the pecans and some flour. Sift the rest of the flour with the salt. Blend the bicarbonate of soda and milk.

3 Beat the butter and sugar together until pale and fluffy. Beat in the eggs, followed by two thirds of the orange zest and the orange-flower water. Gently fold in alternating spoonfuls of flour, milk and apricot mixture until everything is evenly mixed.

4 Spoon the mixture into the prepared tin and bake in the preheated oven for 1¼ hours or until a skewer inserted into the cake comes out clean.

5 For the syrup, gently heat the orange juice, sugar and remaining orange zest in a small heavy-based pan until the sugar has dissolved. Keep warm.

6 Remove the cake from the oven and prick the top here and there with a fine skewer. Spoon over the hot syrup and leave for 10 minutes. Turn out on to a wire rack, peel off the lining paper and leave to cool. Decorate with the pecan nuts and strands of orange zest.

 Oven temperature
160°C/325°F/gas 3

 Baking time
1¼ hours

 Cake tin
1kg (2lb) loaf tin, greased and lined

 Makes
16–20 slices

 Storage
Keeps for 3 weeks

 Freezing
Freezes for 1–2 months

 Step ahead
Soak the apricots overnight

Farmhouse Fruit Cake

An English tea-time treat from the west country, this traditional, lightly fruited cake is reminiscent of days when the whole family sat down together for high tea after the day's hard work was done.

INGREDIENTS

375g (12oz) plain flour

2 tsp baking powder

½ tsp bicarbonate of soda

125g (4oz) butter, cut into pieces

125g (4oz) caster sugar

90ml (6 tbsp) golden syrup, warmed

2 eggs, lightly beaten

250ml (8fl oz) milk

125g (4oz) currants

125g (4oz) sultanas

125g (4oz) chopped mixed peel

1 tsp finely grated lemon zest

caster sugar to decorate

1 Sift the flour, baking powder and bicarbonate of soda together into a large bowl. Add the butter and rub together into a coarse, crumb-like mixture. Stir in the caster sugar.

2 Pour the golden syrup into another bowl. Add the beaten eggs and milk and whisk together well. Stir into the flour mixture together with the dried fruit, mixed peel and grated lemon zest until evenly mixed.

3 Pour the mixture into the prepared tin and bake in the preheated oven for 1½ hours or until a skewer inserted into the cake comes out clean. Remove from the oven, sprinkle with caster sugar and leave in the tin on a wire rack to cool. Turn out, peel off the lining paper and sprinkle with a little more caster sugar to decorate.

 Oven temperature
160°C/325°F/gas 3

 Baking time
1½ hours

 Cake tin
18cm (7in) deep, round tin, greased and lined

 Makes
8 slices

 Storage
Keeps for 1 week

 Freezing
Freezes for 2–3 months

Nut & Seed Cakes

In Europe there is a passion for cakes filled with nuts and seeds. Such cakes need little enrichment; eggs and sugar almost suffice. Flour is rarely added and butter is often omitted as nuts and seeds contain natural oils that impart a fine moist texture, and it is the separated egg whites whipped into a stiff foam that lighten and give the mixture air. These cakes tend not to rise much but their flavour is strong, pure and very distinctive.

CHOPPED WALNUTS *in the mixture keep the cake moist.*

POLISH COFFEE AND WALNUT CAKE
A hint of cocoa adds depth of flavour to this classic cake.

Polish Coffee & Walnut Cake

Maria Wosiek, my Polish friend, helped me take care of my sons when they were young; she was always patient and loving, even when they were very naughty. When we went on holiday she would cook special Polish dishes – borscht, stuffed cabbage, "pierozki" and apple fritters. This was her favourite cake.

INGREDIENTS

For the cake

1 tbsp cocoa powder

4 eggs, separated

100g (3½oz) icing sugar

1 tbsp toasted breadcrumbs, finely ground (see page 45)

1 tbsp coffee-flavoured syrup (see page 153)

180g (6oz) walnuts, finely chopped

For the filling and decoration

½ quantity coffee mousseline buttercream (see page 150)

3 tbsp apricot glaze (see page 149)

1 quantity coffee glacé icing (see page 152)

15 walnut halves

chocolate coffee beans

30g (1oz) chopped walnuts

1 For the cake, blend the cocoa with 1 teaspoon of boiling water. Whisk the egg yolks and icing sugar together in a bowl to the ribbon stage (see page 48).

2 Gently fold the cocoa, breadcrumbs, coffee syrup and walnuts into the egg yolk mixture until evenly mixed.

3 In another bowl, whisk the egg whites into soft peaks. Gently fold into the main mixture, taking care not to knock out the air.

4 Pour the mixture into the prepared tin and bake in the preheated oven for 1 hour. Remove from the oven and leave for 5 minutes. Turn out on to a wire rack and leave to cool.

5 Slice the cake horizontally in half. Sandwich together with the buttercream. Place on a wire rack set over a plate. Brush with the glaze, then pour on the glacé icing and coax over the top and sides (see page 142). Decorate with the walnut halves, coffee beans and chopped walnuts. Leave to set before serving.

 Oven temperature
180°C/350°F/gas 4

 Baking time
1 hour

 Cake tin
22cm (8½in) springform tin, greased and floured

 Makes
12 slices

 Storage
Keeps for 3–4 days

Freezing
Freezes for 1–2 months, undecorated

Step ahead
Prepare the toasted breadcrumbs; make the coffee-flavoured syrup and coffee mousseline buttercream

Engadiner Nusstorte

INGREDIENTS

For the pastry

2 quantities German pastry (see page 94), made with plain flour

For the filling

200g (7oz) caster sugar

250g (8oz) walnuts, coarsely chopped

250ml (8fl oz) double cream

4 tbsp honey, warmed

1 tsp finely grated lemon zest

1 egg white, lightly beaten

1 Make the German pastry (see page 94) and set aside just over half. Roll out the remainder between two sheets of silicone paper into a 20cm (8in) circle. Slide on to a baking sheet and chill until firm. Press the remaining pastry on to the base and up the sides of the prepared tin, using the back of a spoon. Chill until required.

2 For the filling, put the sugar into a large, heavy-based frying pan and heat gently, without stirring, until it has melted and become a pale golden liquid. Immediately take it off the heat and stir in the walnuts. Mix in the cream, honey and lemon zest. Set aside to cool.

3 Spoon the filling into the pastry case and level the top. Peel the paper off the chilled pastry and lay over the filling. Press the edges together well to seal. Prick the top with a fork and brush with the egg white.

4 Bake in the preheated oven for 25–30 minutes until golden. Remove from the oven and leave in the tin on a wire rack to cool. Carefully lift out of the tin and cut into very thin slices to serve.

 Oven temperature
200°C/400°F/gas 6

 Baking time
25–30 minutes

 Cake tin
22cm (8½in) straight-sided, loose-bottomed Victoria Sandwich tin or springform tin, greased

 Makes
12–16 slices

 Storage
Keeps for 1–2 weeks

 Freezing
Freezes for 2–3 months

Poppy Seed Strudel

Poppy seed pastries feature strongly in the Christmas baking traditions of Hungary, Austria, Germany and Poland, and each country has its own variations. Pound the poppy seeds coarsely with a pestle and mortar, or grind in an electric coffee grinder, before using. However, take care not to grind them too finely or the oils will be released, making the seeds greasy and bitter tasting.

INGREDIENTS

For the pastry

125g (4oz) plain flour, sifted

125g (4oz) self-raising flour, sifted

150g (5oz) butter, cut into pieces

60g (2oz) caster sugar

30g (1oz) icing sugar, sifted

1 tsp finely grated lemon zest

1 egg, lightly beaten

For the filling

125g (4oz) poppy seeds

125ml (4fl oz) clear honey

30g (1oz) butter

90g (3oz) walnuts, finely chopped

90g (3oz) raisins

For the decoration

1 egg white, lightly beaten

2 tsp caster sugar

icing sugar

1 Make the pastry following the method for pâte sucrée (see page 55). Chill for 1 hour.

2 For the filling, coarsely grind the poppy seeds in a clean electric coffee grinder. Put the honey and butter into a pan and melt over a low heat. Stir in the poppy seeds, walnuts and raisins and cook for 1 minute. Leave to cool slightly.

3 Allow the pastry to come back to room temperature. Knead briefly until smooth. Roll out on a lightly floured surface into a 35x25cm (14x10in) rectangle. Spread over the warm filling to within 2.5cm (1in) of the edge. Roll up from one long edge and pinch the ends together to seal.

4 Lay the roll on the prepared baking sheet, seam-side down, brush with the egg white and sprinkle with the sugar. Bake in the preheated oven for 25–30 minutes or until golden.

5 Remove from the oven and rest for 5 minutes. Transfer to a wire rack and leave to cool. Dust with icing sugar and cut into thin slices once cold.

 Oven temperature
190°C/375°F/gas 5

 Baking time
25–30 minutes

 Cake tin
35x25cm (14x10in) baking sheet, greased with butter

 Makes
20 slices

 Storage
Keeps for 1 week

 Step ahead
Make the pastry and chill for 1 hour

Nun's Seed Cake

Here is a recipe for caraway seed cake adapted from Hannah Glasse's The Art of Cookery Made Plain & Easy, written in 1747. I was delighted to discover that the flavours of caraway and orange-flower water enhance each other.

INGREDIENTS

200g (7oz) self-raising flour

1 tsp ground cinnamon

200g (7oz) butter

150g (5oz) caster sugar

3 eggs

2 tsp orange-flower or rose water

2–3 tsp caraway seeds

1 Sift the flour and cinnamon together twice into a bowl and set aside.

2 In another bowl, beat the butter until soft and creamy. Add the caster sugar and beat together for 3–4 minutes until pale and fluffy.

3 Beat in the eggs, one at a time, adding a little of the sifted flour and cinnamon with the last egg if the mixture begins to curdle.

4 Carefully fold the remaining flour into the main mixture, followed by the orange-flower water or rose water and the caraway seeds, until everything is evenly mixed.

5 Spoon the mixture into the prepared tin and lightly level the surface. Bake in the preheated oven for 45 minutes–1 hour or until richly golden and a skewer inserted into the cake comes out clean.

6 Remove from the oven and leave to rest in the tin for 10 minutes. Turn out on to a wire rack and leave to cool.

 Oven temperature
180°C/350°F/gas 4

 Baking time
45 minutes–1 hour

 Cake tin
1kg (2lb) loaf tin, greased and base-lined

 Makes
16 slices

 Storage
Keeps for 4–5 days

 Freezing
Freezes for 1–2 months

Hazelnut Cake

Passover, or Pesach, commemorates the exodus of the Jews from Egypt during the rule of the Pharaohs. By Jewish law, it is forbidden to eat any baked goods containing raising agents or flour, so cakes made with nuts are popular. The texture of this cake is light yet deliciously nutty and it has a distinctive orange flavour. It tastes even better covered in a layer of melted plain chocolate (see step 4 for the Whipped Almond Cake below).

INGREDIENTS

180g (6oz) caster sugar

4 eggs, separated

1 tbsp drinking chocolate powder

1 tbsp finely grated orange zest

200g (7oz) roasted hazelnuts, finely chopped (see page 45)

3 tbsp matzo meal or toasted white breadcrumbs, finely ground (see page 45)

2 tsp orange juice

icing sugar to decorate

1 Set aside 4 tablespoons of the sugar. Whisk the remainder with the egg yolks and drinking chocolate to the ribbon stage (see page 48). Whisk in the zest.

2 In another bowl, whisk the egg whites into soft peaks. Whisk in the reserved sugar until they form slightly stiffer peaks (see page 49). Stir 2 large spoonfuls of the egg white into the egg yolk mixture to loosen the texture.

3 Mix together the hazelnuts and matzo meal or toasted breadcrumbs. Fold into the egg yolk mixture. Gently fold in the remaining egg white taking care not to knock out the air. Fold in the orange juice.

4 Spoon the mixture into the prepared tin and lightly level the surface. Bake in the preheated oven for 55 minutes, or until a skewer inserted into the cake comes out clean. Cover with a domed piece of foil towards the end of the cooking time if it starts to over-brown.

5 Remove from the oven and leave to rest for 10 minutes. Turn out on to a wire rack and leave to cool. Peel off the lining paper. Dust with icing sugar and serve with whipped cream.

Oven temperature
180°C/350°F/gas 4

Baking time
55 minutes

Cake tin
22cm (8½in) springform tin, greased and lined

Makes
12 slices

Storage
Keeps for 1 week

Freezing
Freezes for 1–2 months

Step ahead
Prepare the roasted hazelnuts, and toasted breadcrumbs if using

Whipped Almond Cake

This cake is very quick and easy to prepare. It contains no flour: air is the only raising agent, so be sure to whisk the mixture well and then fold in the almonds and egg whites swiftly but gently. This is used as a delicious base sponge in the Esterházy Cream Torte (see page 71).

INGREDIENTS

For the cake

6 eggs

150g (5oz) caster sugar

1 tsp finely grated orange zest

150g (5oz) ground almonds

For the decoration

4 tbsp apricot glaze (see page 149)

200g (7oz) plain chocolate

1 For the cake, separate 4 of the eggs and set aside 2 tablespoons of the sugar. Whisk the remaining sugar with the egg yolks, whole eggs and orange zest to the ribbon stage (see page 48). Gradually stir in the almonds until evenly mixed.

2 In another bowl, whisk the egg whites into soft peaks. Whisk in the reserved sugar until they form slightly stiffer peaks (see page 49). Gently fold into the main mixture, taking care not to knock out the air.

3 Pour the mixture into the prepared tin and bake in the preheated oven for 1 hour or until a skewer inserted into the cake comes out clean. Remove from the oven and leave to rest for 5 minutes. Turn out on to a wire rack and leave to cool.

4 Peel the lining paper off the base of the cake and place it, right-side up, on to a wire rack set over a plate. Brush the top and sides with the apricot glaze. Melt the chocolate (see page 44), then cool slightly until thickened but not set. While still warm, pour the chocolate on to the centre of the cake and spread evenly over the top and sides with a small palette knife (see page 142). Leave to set before serving.

Oven temperature
160°C/325°F/gas 3

Baking time
1 hour

Cake tin
23cm (9in) springform tin, greased and base-lined

Makes
12 slices

Storage
Keeps for 1 week

Freezing
Freezes for 1–2 months, undecorated

Step ahead
Make the apricot glaze

Coconut Layer Cake

Coconut cakes are often very sweet and heavy. I include soured cream which helps to lighten the cake, makes it fluffier and brings out its distinct coconut taste. The sharp, fresh flavour of the cranberry jelly filling complements the cake well, particularly when it is accompanied by a sweet cream cheese frosting. If you have not used a fresh coconut before, the steps below show you how to extract the water and the flesh. (See page 23 for illustration.)

INGREDIENTS

For the cake

180g (6oz) fresh coconut, finely grated (see below)
180g (6oz) butter
375g (12oz) caster sugar
3 eggs
300ml (½ pint) soured cream
250g (8oz) self-raising flour, sifted
125ml (4fl oz) fresh coconut water

For the filling and decoration

150ml (10 tbsp) cranberry jelly
180g (6oz) cream cheese
125g (4oz) unsalted butter, softened
½ tsp vanilla extract
500g (1lb) icing sugar, sifted
toasted coconut shavings (see below)

1 For the cake, set aside 75g (2½oz) of the grated coconut. Spread the remainder on a baking tray and bake in the preheated oven for 15 minutes, stirring every now and then, until it is dry and lightly golden. Leave to cool.

2 Beat the butter and sugar together until pale and fluffy. Beat in the eggs, one at a time. Gently stir in the soured cream, followed by the flour, the fresh coconut water and the roasted coconut until evenly mixed.

3 Spoon the mixture into the prepared tins and bake in the preheated oven for 35 minutes or until a skewer inserted into each cake comes out clean. Remove from the oven and leave to rest in the tins for 10 minutes. Turn out on to a wire rack, carefully peel off the lining paper and leave to cool.

TO FINISH THE CAKE

1 Slice each cake horizontally in half. Sandwich each one back together with 5 tablespoons of the cranberry jelly.

2 For the frosting, beat the cream cheese, butter and vanilla extract together until smooth. Gradually beat in the icing sugar. Sandwich the two cakes together with 5–6 tablespoons of the frosting.

3 Spread the remaining cream cheese frosting evenly over the top and sides of the cake, then coat with the reserved grated fresh coconut (see page 143). Decorate the top of the cake with the toasted coconut shavings (see steps 3–4 below).

 Oven temperature
180°C/350°F/gas 4

 Baking time
35 minutes

 Cake tins
Two 22cm (8½in) Victoria Sandwich tins, greased and base-lined

 Makes
12 slices

 Storage
Keeps for 2–3 days in the refrigerator

 Freezing
Freezes for 1–2 months, undecorated

Step ahead
Prepare the fresh coconut and the toasted shavings (see steps 1–4 below)

Preparing a Fresh Coconut

1 *Pierce two of the eyes with a skewer. Drain the water through a muslin-lined sieve into a jug. Bake the coconut at 160°C/325°F/gas 3 for 20 minutes.*

2 *Remove the coconut from the oven and cool slightly. Then wrap in a cloth and sharply tap the shell with a small hammer. It will crack open quite easily.*

3 *Separate the husk from the flesh and discard it. Peel the brown skin off most of the flesh with a potato peeler and grate finely for the cake.*

4 *Peel the remaining flesh into long, thin strips with a potato peeler. Spread on a baking sheet and toast under a medium grill for 3–4 minutes or until golden.*

Spanish Almond Sponge

Almonds, honey and sugar are extremely popular ingredients in Spanish cakes and sweetmeats. Originating in early convent kitchens for the celebration of Christmas, such cakes are now eaten throughout the year. Brush the top of the cake with a little warmed honey before decorating with the flaked almonds and icing sugar if you wish.

INGREDIENTS

For the cake

75g (2½oz) butter

180g (6oz) caster sugar

1 tsp finely grated orange zest

2 eggs, lightly beaten

90g (3oz) plain flour, sifted

90g (3oz) ground almonds

2 tsp brandy or Grand Marnier

30g (1oz) flaked almonds

For the filling

150ml (¼ pint) double cream

2 tbsp caster sugar

1 tbsp brandy or Grand Marnier

45g (1½oz) toasted flaked almonds

For the decoration

30g (1oz) toasted flaked almonds

icing sugar

1 Beat the butter, sugar and orange zest together until pale and fluffy. Gradually beat in the eggs. Fold in alternating spoonfuls of flour and ground almonds, until everything is evenly mixed. Fold in the brandy or Grand Marnier.

2 Pour the mixture into the prepared tin, sprinkle with the flaked almonds and bake in the preheated oven for about 40 minutes or until a skewer inserted into the cake comes out clean. Remove from the oven and leave to rest in the tin for 5 minutes. Turn out on to a wire rack and leave to cool.

3 For the filling, whip the cream, sugar and brandy or Grand Marnier into soft peaks. Fold in the almonds.

4 Slice the cake horizontally in half. Sandwich the layers together with the almond cream filling and transfer to a plate. Sprinkle the top of the cake with the remaining toasted flaked almonds, then dust lightly with icing sugar to decorate.

Oven temperature
180°C/350°F/gas 4

Baking time
40 minutes

Cake tin
19cm (7½in) springform tin, greased and floured

Makes
8 slices

Storage
Keeps for 2–3 days

Freezing
Freezes for 1–2 months

Cheesecakes

Traditionally made for festive occasions, the first cheesecakes were simply soft cheeses perfumed with spices and flower waters, then wrapped in thin pastry cases and baked. Today baked cheesecakes are gloriously rich and made from various curd or cream cheeses, eggs, sugar and flavourings. They should be dense without being cloying. Contemporary cheesecakes can also be fruity, cold-set and refreshingly light.

Mango & Passion Fruit Cheesecake

This chilled cheesecake makes a stunning dinner-party dessert. The fruit gives both tempting colour and intense and aromatic flavour to counterbalance the richness of the Italian soft cheese.

Special Ingredients

Fresh mango

Passion fruit

Kiwi fruit

Mango, passion fruit and kiwi fruit add colour and flavour to this fresh fruited cheesecake.

Digestive biscuits make a delicious base for cheesecakes and are crushed easily in a sealed plastic bag.

Ground cinnamon gives a subtle flavour to the biscuit base, and complements the flavour of the mango perfectly.

Nutmeg adds a warm spicy note. Grate it fresh for the recipe, just before adding.

Apricot jam subtly flavours and helps to bind the biscuit crumb base.

Gelatine is sprinkled on to cold liquid, then gently heated until clear. It lightly sets the rich cheese filling.

Making the cheesecake

The lightly spiced, crushed-biscuit base contrasts well with the creamy smooth topping, exotically flavoured with refreshing passion fruit juice and pieces of mango.

INGREDIENTS

For the base

180g (6oz) digestive biscuits, crushed

½ tsp ground cinnamon

pinch of freshly grated nutmeg

75g (2½ oz) butter

1 tbsp apricot jam

For the filling

425g (14oz) can mango slices

1½ tbsp powdered gelatine

6 passion fruit

1 orange

4 eggs, separated

150g (5oz) caster sugar

200g (7oz) mascarpone cheese

200ml (7fl oz) double cream, lightly whipped

For the decoration

2 fresh mangoes, peeled and sliced

1–2 kiwi fruit, peeled and sliced

pulp from 1 passion fruit

1 For the base, mix the biscuits and spices together. Melt the butter and the apricot jam. Mix into the biscuits and then spoon into the prepared tin. Press evenly on to the base with a spoon, then chill.

2 For the filling, drain the canned mangoes and spoon 90ml (3fl oz) of the juice into a heatproof bowl. Sprinkle over the gelatine and leave to stand for 5 minutes. Sit the bowl in a pan of simmering water and leave until clear (see page 45). Remove and set aside.

3 Decorate the sides of the prepared tin with 5–6 of the mango slices. Roughly chop the remainder. Halve the passion fruit, scoop the pulp into a sieve and press the juice into a bowl. Zest and juice the orange and stir into the passion fruit juice with the chopped mango and dissolved gelatine.

4 Whisk the egg yolks and sugar together until thick and mousse-like. Whisk in the mascarpone cheese. Stir in the fruit mixture and set aside until it starts to thicken and set.

5 Whisk the egg whites into soft peaks (see page 47). Quickly fold the whipped cream into the setting cheese mixture, followed by the egg whites. Pour into the tin and chill for at least 5 hours or until set.

6 Remove from the tin and transfer to a plate. Decorate the top with the mango and kiwi fruit slices. Spoon the passion fruit pulp into the centre.

Cake tin
22cm (8½ in) springform tin, greased lightly with vegetable oil and base-lined

Makes
10–12 slices

Storage
Keeps for 3 days

Warning
This recipe contains raw eggs (see page 9)

16th-Century Maids of Honour

Anne Boleyn, who was a Maid of Honour at the court of King Henry VIII in 1552, and later became one of his ill-fated wives, reputedly baked these cheese tartlets to tempt His Majesty. He seemed to approve, for he named them in her honour. Take care not to overfill the tartlet cases, or the mixture will run over the sides as they bake.

INGREDIENTS

For the pastry cases

1 quantity pâte brisée pastry (see page 54)

For the filling

90g (3oz) butter, softened

125g (4oz) curd cheese

2 egg yolks

90g (3oz) caster sugar

1 tsp finely grated lemon zest

60g (2oz) ground almonds

1 tsp orange-flower water

pinch of freshly grated nutmeg

2 tbsp lemon juice

75g (2½ oz) candied peel, finely chopped

1 Allow the pastry to come back to room temperature.

Knead briefly until smooth. Roll out on a lightly floured surface and cut out twenty-four 7cm (3in) circles using a fluted biscuit cutter. Press into the prepared tray, prick with a fork and chill for 20 minutes.

2 For the filling, beat together the butter and curd cheese until smooth. Beat in the egg yolks, sugar, zest, almonds and orange-flower water. Stir in the nutmeg and lemon juice.

3 Drop a little candied peel into each pastry case. Spoon in some filling until just over half full. Bake in the preheated oven for 20–25 minutes. Remove from the oven and cool in the tin.

 Oven temperature
200°C/400°F/gas 6

 Baking time
20–25 minutes

 Cake tins
Two deep patty tins, greased

 Makes
24 tartlets

 Storage
Keep for 1–2 days

 Freezing
Freeze for 1 month

 Step ahead
Make the pastry and chill for 1 hour

Pêches à la Melba Cheesecake

Dame Nellie Melba, the Australian opera singer, was a regular visitor to London's Savoy Hotel during the 1890s. Auguste Escoffier, the chef at the time, dedicated a dessert of peaches, ice-cream and raspberry purée to the renowned artiste. Here is a further tribute to them both. (See page 17 for illustration.)

INGREDIENTS

For the base

1 quantity pâte sucrée pastry (see page 55)

For the filling

60g (2oz) ground almonds

1 tbsp caster sugar

750g (1½ lb) ripe fresh peaches, halved, stoned and peeled

300g (10oz) cream cheese

90ml (3fl oz) soured cream

60g (2oz) caster sugar

3 eggs, separated

1 tsp finely grated lemon zest

For the decoration

10 fresh raspberries

mint sprigs

icing sugar

1 quantity raspberry sauce (see page 149)

1 Allow the pastry to come back to room temperature. Knead briefly until smooth and roll out on a lightly floured surface into a 25cm (10in) circle. Press on to the base and slightly up the sides of the prepared tin. Prick all over with a fork and bake blind for 10 minutes (see page

56). Lower the oven temperature and bake for another 10 minutes. Uncover and bake for a further 10 minutes. Remove from the oven and leave to cool. Lower the oven temperature once more.

2 For the filling, mix together the almonds and sugar and spread evenly over the pastry. Arrange the peach halves on top.

3 Beat the cheese, cream and sugar together until smooth. Mix in the egg yolks and lemon zest. Whisk the egg whites into soft peaks. Stir 2 spoonfuls into the cheese mixture, then gently fold in the remainder.

4 Pour the mixture into the tin and bake for 1¼ hours. Cover with domed foil halfway through to prevent over-browning. Turn off the oven and leave inside until cold.

5 Remove from the tin and top with the raspberries and mint. Dust with icing sugar and serve with the raspberry sauce.

 Oven temperature
200°C/400°F/gas 6, then 180°C/350°F/gas 4 for the base; 160°C/325°F/gas 3 for the cheesecake

 Baking time
30 minutes for the base; 1¼ hours for the cheesecake

 Cake tin
24cm (9½in) springform tin, greased

 **Makes**
8–10 slices

 Storage
Keeps for 2–3 days

 Step ahead
Make the pastry and chill for 1 hour; prepare the fresh peaches; make the raspberry sauce

Hoboken Cinnamon Cheesecake

My youngest son, Jeremy, owns "Oddfellow's Rest", a bar and restaurant in Hoboken, New Jersey, USA. This is the most popular cake on the menu. The recipe was given to me by his chef, Wayne Haney.

INGREDIENTS

For the filling

75g (2½oz) raisins

2 tbsp dark rum

1kg (2lb) curd cheese

125g (4oz) granulated sugar

2 tsp cornflour, sifted

½ tsp vanilla extract

2 tbsp ground cinnamon

2 large eggs (size 1)

2 egg yolks

250ml (8fl oz) soured cream

For the base

180g (6oz) digestive biscuits, crushed

2 tbsp cocoa powder

125g (4oz) light soft brown sugar

60g (2oz) butter, melted and cooled

1 small egg white, lightly beaten

1 Soak the raisins in the rum for 30 minutes then drain.

2 For the base, put the crushed biscuits, cocoa and sugar into a bowl. Stir in the butter and egg white until everything is well mixed. Press evenly on to the base of the prepared tin.

3 For the filling, beat the curd cheese and sugar together until smooth. Beat in the cornflour, vanilla and cinnamon, followed by the whole eggs and egg yolks, one at a time. Dry the raisins well and fold in with the soured cream. Pour into the tin.

4 Bake in the preheated oven for 10 minutes. Lower the temperature and bake for a further 1 hour 40 minutes until set, covering with a domed piece of foil if it starts to over-brown. Turn off the oven and leave inside until cold. Remove from the tin to serve.

Oven temperature
200°C/400°F/gas 6, then 150°C/300°F/gas 2

Baking time
10 minutes at the higher temperature, then 1 hour 40 minutes at the lower temperature

Cake tin
24cm (9½in) springform tin, greased

Makes
10 slices

Storage
Keeps for 2–3 days

Freezing
Freezes for 1–2 months

Golden Baked Cheesecake

A traditional baked cheesecake, this has a rich yet delicate texture. The cake collapses in the centre as it cools and sometimes cracks, but don't worry, that's exactly the way it should be. (See page 16 for illustration.)

INGREDIENTS

For the filling

60g (2oz) raisins

2 tbsp dark rum

400g (13oz) curd cheese

125ml (4fl oz) soured cream

2 eggs, separated

1 egg yolk

125g (4oz) caster sugar

1 tbsp vanilla sugar

2 tsp finely grated lemon zest

icing sugar to decorate

For the base

1 quantity pâte brisée pastry (see page 54)

1 Soak the raisins in the rum overnight in a covered bowl.

2 Allow the pastry to come back to room temperature. Knead briefly until smooth. Roll out half on a lightly floured surface into a 23cm (9in) circle. Press on to the base and slightly up the sides of the prepared tin. Prick all over with a fork and bake in the preheated oven for 10–15 minutes. Remove from the oven and leave to cool. Lower the oven temperature.

3 Roll out the remaining pastry into a 2.5cm (1in) long band. Cut in half lengthways. Use to line the sides of the tin, pressing them on to the base to seal.

4 For the filling, beat the cheese, cream, egg yolks, caster and vanilla sugars, and zest together until thick. In another bowl, whisk the egg whites into soft peaks (see page 47). Stir 2 spoonfuls into the cheese mixture, then gently fold in the rest. Fold in the raisins.

5 Pour the mixture into the tin and bake for 1 hour. Turn off the oven and leave inside until cold. Remove from the tin and dust with icing sugar to serve.

Oven temperature
200°C/400°F/gas 6 for the base; 180°C/350°F/gas 4 for the cheesecake

Baking time
10–15 minutes for the base; 1 hour for the cheesecake

Cake tin
22cm (8½in) springform tin, greased

Makes
10–12 slices

Storage
Keeps for 2–3 days

Freezing
Freezes for 1–2 months

Step ahead
Soak the raisins; make the pastry and chill for 1 hour

Meringues

Egg whites, the simplest of ingredients, are vigorously whisked into an airy froth and then combined with sugar to make a thick and glossy foam, which is shaped and then baked very gently until crisp, dry and evenly coloured. The resulting confection melts in the mouth to a delicious sugary nothingness and wonderfully complements all the finest cake creams, fruit and fillings, and blends delectably with nuts. Plain meringues keep well so if you have some in store you can produce a tempting dessert in moments.

Simple Meringues

Meringues are easy to make, and when covered with whipped cream and other sumptuous ingredients, such as soft fruit or chocolate, they must surely be an all-time favourite. Remember that eggs should always be at room temperature before starting preparation. Simple Meringues can be stored in an airtight tin or wrapped in aluminium foil.

INGREDIENTS

2 egg whites

pinch of cream of tartar

125g (4oz) caster sugar, sifted

chopped nuts or granulated sugar

150ml (¼ pint) double cream, whipped

fresh strawberries to decorate

1 Put the egg whites into a large, clean bowl and whisk slowly until they become thick and frothy. Add the cream of tartar and continue to whisk more quickly until they form stiff peaks (see page 49).

2 Sift over half the caster sugar and continue whisking until the mixture is stiff and glossy. The remaining sugar can be added in one of two ways. Either sift over the sugar, half at a time, and gently fold it in, or, for a firmer meringue which is particularly good for piping (see page 49), whisk in the rest of the sugar a little at a time.

FOR SIMPLE MERINGUES
For individual meringues, scoop out 10 large spoonfuls of the meringue mixture and push them on to the prepared baking sheet, about 2cm (¾in) apart (see page 49). Alternatively, spoon the mixture into a piping bag fitted with a 1cm (½in) plain or star nozzle and pipe 7cm (3in) mounds on to the baking sheet. Sprinkle with a few chopped roasted hazelnuts, pistachio nuts, flaked almonds or a little granulated sugar if you wish.

FOR MERINGUE DISCS
To make a meringue disc, mark the prepared baking sheet with a 22cm (8½in) circle as a guideline. Spoon the mixture on to the baking sheet and spread out within the marked circle to a thickness of about 2cm (¾in). (Remember the meringue will expand during cooking.) Alternatively, spoon the mixture into a piping bag fitted with a 1cm (½in) plain nozzle and, starting in the centre of the marked circle, pipe in a spiral pattern to form a flat disc (see page 49). Sprinkle lightly with a little granulated sugar if wished.

TO COOK THE MERINGUE
Bake in the preheated oven until crisp and dry (see page 49). The time taken will depend on the size of the meringue. Allow 50 minutes–1 hour for individual meringues and about 1½–2 hours for a meringue disc. Switch off the oven and leave the meringues inside until completely cold. Lift off the lining paper.

TO FINISH THE MERINGUE
Sandwich individual meringues together with the whipped cream and decorate with the fresh strawberries.

Oven temperature
120°C/250°F/gas ½

Baking time
50 minutes–1 hour for individual meringues; 1½–2 hours for meringue discs

Cake tin
One or two flat baking sheets, lined with silicone paper

Makes
10 individual meringues (5 pairs), or one 22cm (8½in) meringue disc

Storage
Keep for 1–2 months, unfilled, wrapped in aluminium foil or stored in an airtight tin

Special Toppings for Meringue Discs

Cranberry and Orange Meringue

Cook 250g (8oz) cranberries with 1 teaspoon finely grated orange zest, 2 strips orange peel and 125ml (4fl oz) water for 10 minutes. Remove the orange strips. Stir in 125g (4oz) caster sugar, then cool. Spread a 22cm (8½in) meringue disc with 300ml (½ pint) whipped double cream. Spoon over the cranberries. Decorate with fine orange shreds.

Chocolate Cream Meringue

Whip 300ml (½ pint) double cream with 2 tablespoons caster sugar and 2 tablespoons Cointreau or dark rum. Spread over a 22cm (8½in) meringue disc and sprinkle with 100g (3½oz) grated plain chocolate.

Autumn Fruit Meringue

Spread a 22cm (8½in) meringue disc with 300ml (½ pint) whipped double cream. Sprinkle with 500g (1lb) mixed fruits such as blackberries, loganberries, sliced plums, black grapes and blueberries.

Chestnut Meringue

Beat together 300g (10oz) unsweetened chestnut purée, 60g (2oz) caster sugar and 1 tablespoon dark rum. Stir in 4 tablespoons lightly whipped double cream. Spoon into a piping bag fitted with a 5mm (¼in) plain nozzle. Pipe long strands over the top of a 22cm (8½in) meringue disc, sprinkle with thin slices of marrons glacés and dust lightly with icing sugar to decorate.

Summer Berry Vacherin

A meringue vacherin probably holds pride of place as the most desirable dessert gâteau. The light and crisp sugary layers brimming with richly coloured berries combined with liqueur-laced fruity cream are quite irresistible. (See page 21 for illustration.)

INGREDIENTS

For the meringues

4 quantities Simple Meringues mixture (see page 112)

granulated sugar

For the filling

180g (6oz) fresh raspberries

90g (3oz) caster sugar, sifted

180g (6oz) fresh strawberries

1.25 litres (2 pints) double cream

90ml (6 tbsp) Grand Marnier

For the decoration

90g (3oz) fresh blueberries

125g (4oz) mixed fresh redcurrants, blackcurrants and white currants

125g (4oz) fresh strawberries, halved

1 kiwi fruit, peeled, sliced and halved

90g (3oz) fresh blackberries

1 Mark a 22cm (8½in) circle on to each prepared baking sheet. Make two quantities of the meringue mixture and spread out equally within the marked circles (see page 49).

2 Make another two quantities of the meringue mixture and spoon into a piping bag fitted with a 1cm (½in) star nozzle. Pipe a line of 2.5cm (1in) stars around the edge of each disc. On one disc, pipe a second row of stars over the first to give a raised edge.

3 Sprinkle each disc with some granulated sugar. Bake in the preheated oven for 2½–3 hours until crisp and dry. Switch off the oven and leave inside until cold.

4 For the filling, crush the raspberries with 30g (1oz) of sugar. Chop the strawberries and press through a plastic sieve or purée in a liquidizer. Stir in 30g (1oz) of the sugar. Whip the cream, remaining sugar and Grand Marnier into soft peaks. Mix one third with the crushed raspberries, another third with the puréed strawberries and leave the remainder plain.

5 Lift the the meringues off the lining paper. Put one flat disc on a plate and spread with the raspberry cream. Cover with the second flat disc and spread over the strawberry cream. Cover with the last disc and spoon the plain cream into the centre. Arrange the fruit on top and serve within 1–2 hours.

Oven temperature
110°C/225°F/gas ¼

Baking time
2½–3 hours

Cake tins
Three flat baking sheets, lined with silicone paper

Makes
10–12 slices

Storage
The meringue discs keep for 1–2 months, wrapped in aluminium foil or stored in an airtight tin; best eaten within 1–2 hours of assembly

Nectarine Pavlova

Anna Pavlova was the famous Russian ballerina for whom "The Dying Swan" was created. This lovely, soft meringue is reputed to have been created in Australia in her honour.

INGREDIENTS

For the meringue

4 egg whites

250g (8oz) caster sugar

1 tsp vanilla extract

1 tsp white wine vinegar or lemon juice

2 tsp cornflour

For the topping

3 nectarines, 2 peaches and 250g (8oz) cherries

2 tbsp vanilla sugar

450ml (¾ pint) double cream

1½ tbsp Grand Marnier

1 Mark a 23cm (9in) circle or oval on to the prepared baking sheet. For the meringue, whisk the egg whites into stiff peaks. Gradually whisk in the sugar, 1 tablespoon at a time, until they form a stiff, glossy meringue (see page 49). Whisk in the vanilla extract, vinegar or lemon juice and cornflour.

2 Spoon the mixture on to the prepared baking sheet and spread within the marked circle (see page 49). Make a slight dip in the centre of the meringue so that the outside edge is slightly higher. Bake in the preheated oven for 1–1¼ hours or until pale biscuit-coloured, hard to the touch on the outside and marshmallow-like in the centre. Turn off the oven and leave the Pavlova inside until cold. Remove from the oven and carefully lift off the lining paper.

3 For the topping, halve, stone and slice the nectarines and peaches and stone the cherries. Put into a shallow dish and sprinkle with the vanilla sugar. Whip the double cream with the Grand Marnier into soft peaks.

4 Just before serving, spread the cream over the top of the Pavlova and pile the fruit decoratively on top.

VARIATION
Tropical Fruit Pavlova
For the topping, use 750g (1½lb) prepared mixed fresh tropical fruit such as pineapple, kiwi fruit, banana, pawpaw and mango. Prepare and assemble following the main recipe above, using caster sugar not vanilla sugar.

 Oven temperature
150°C/300°F/gas 2

 Baking time
1–1¼ hours

 Cake tin
Flat baking sheet, lined with silicone paper

 Makes
6–8 slices

Storage
Keeps for 2–3 days, undecorated

Torta di Pinoli

Pine nuts are harvested from the stone pine, which is native to south-west Europe. The nut is commonly used in Arab cuisine and was introduced to Italy by early travellers. Pine nuts can be eaten raw but take on a better flavour when roasted, as in this delicious pine nut cake. They should be used while fresh as they turn rancid after only three or four months. (See page 20 for illustration.)

INGREDIENTS

200g (7oz) pine nuts

3 egg whites

225g (7½oz) caster sugar

1 tbsp lemon juice

300ml (½ pint) double cream

icing sugar to decorate

1 Spread the pine nuts on a baking tray and roast in the preheated oven for 4–5 minutes. Cool, then set aside 2 tablespoons of nuts and finely chop the rest. Lower the oven temperature.

2 Mark a 23cm (9in) circle on to each prepared baking sheet. Whisk the egg whites into stiff peaks. Gradually whisk in the sugar until they form a stiff, glossy meringue (see page 49). Gently fold in the chopped pine nuts and lemon juice.

3 Spoon the meringue into a piping bag fitted with a 1cm (½in) plain nozzle. Pipe a disc on to each prepared baking sheet (see page 49) and bake for 45–50 minutes. Remove from the oven, lift off the paper and leave to cool on a wire rack.

4 Whip the cream into soft peaks and use to sandwich together the two discs. Sprinkle the cake with the reserved pine nuts and dust with icing sugar.

 Oven temperature
200°C/400°F/gas 6; then
160°C/325°F/gas 3

 Baking time
45–50 minutes

 Cake tins
Two flat baking sheets, lined with silicone paper

 Makes
8 slices

 Storage
Keeps for 1–2 days

 Step ahead
Roast the pine nuts

Mocha Tranche

A layer cake with a difference: crisp rectangular layers of mocha-flavoured meringue are sandwiched together with coffee liqueur-flavoured cream and decorated with delicious melt-in-the-mouth meringue batons.

INGREDIENTS

For the meringue

2 quantities Simple Meringues mixture (see page 112)

2 tbsp cocoa powder

4 tsp instant coffee powder

For the filling and decoration

600ml (1 pint) double cream

1 tbsp caster sugar

2–3 tbsp Tia Maria

cocoa powder

1 Mark three 30x10cm (12x 4in) rectangles on to three of the prepared baking sheets.

2 Make the meringue mixture (see page 112). Mix the cocoa and coffee powder together, sift over the meringue mixture and whisk in until everything is evenly mixed.

3 For the meringue batons, spoon 2 large spoonfuls of the mixture into a piping bag fitted with a 5mm (¼in) plain nozzle. Pipe 7.5cm (3in) lines on to the unmarked baking sheet.

4 For the meringue layers, divide the remaining mixture between the prepared baking sheets and spread out evenly within the marked rectangles (see page 49).

5 Bake the meringue batons in the preheated oven for 45 minutes–1 hour and bake the rectangles for 1½–2 hours until crisp and dry. Remove from the oven and leave to cool on wire racks. Lift off the lining paper.

6 For the filling, whip the cream, caster sugar and Tia Maria into soft peaks. Put one meringue rectangle on a serving plate and spread with a quarter of the cream. Repeat twice more, ending with a layer of cream.

7 Spoon the remaining whipped cream into a piping bag fitted with a 1cm (½in) star nozzle. Pipe in a shell design around the top edge of the Tranche (see page 145). Arrange the meringue batons down the centre and dust with cocoa powder just before serving.

 Oven temperature
120°C/250°F/gas ½

 Baking time
45 minutes–1 hour for the meringue batons, 1½–2 hours for the meringue rectangles

 Cake tins
Four flat baking sheets, lined with silicone paper

 Makes
10 slices

 Storage
Best eaten as soon as it is made

Japonais

This classic French pastry is usually seen in the pâtissier's shop window. Instantly recognizable, each small, flat disc has a single roasted nut set in the middle of the finely chopped nut topping. It looks difficult to make but is really quite simple. While almonds and a mocha filling are traditional, this larger version is made with roasted hazelnuts (see page 45) and filled with chocolate ganache. (See page 20 for illustration.)

INGREDIENTS

For the Japonais

150g (5oz) caster sugar

100g (3½ oz) roasted hazelnuts, finely ground (see page 45)

45g (1½ oz) icing sugar

4 tsp potato flour

4 egg whites

For the filling and decoration

1 quantity chocolate ganache (see page 151)

4 tbsp roasted hazelnuts, finely chopped

8 whole roasted hazelnuts

1 Mark two 24cm (9½ in) circles on the prepared baking sheets. Mix half the caster sugar with the hazelnuts, icing sugar and potato flour.

2 Whisk the egg whites into soft peaks. Gradually whisk in the remaining caster sugar until they form a stiff, glossy meringue (see page 49). Fold in the nut and sugar mixture until everything is evenly mixed.

3 Spead the mixture equally within the marked circles (see page 49) and bake in the preheated oven for 1 hour. Remove from the oven and leave to cool on a wire rack. Lift off the lining paper.

4 Spread half the ganache over the base of one meringue disc. Cover with the second disc, smooth-side up. Spread the remaining ganache over the top and sides of the cake.

5 Press most of the chopped nuts on to the sides (see page 143), arrange the whole nuts around the top and sprinkle the centre with the remaining nuts.

Oven temperature
160°C/325°F/gas 3

Baking time
1 hour

Cake tins
Two flat baking sheets, lined with silicone paper

Makes
12 slices

Storage
Keeps for 4–5 days

Freezing
Freezes for 1–2 months

Step ahead
Prepare the roasted hazelnuts; make the chocolate ganache

Lemon Meringue Pie

A fine combination of contrasting flavours is created in this sharp and tart lemon cream with a sweet, crisp pastry, topped with a soft cloud of meringue. It is not unlike the Elizabethan sweet-filled "royal pye", which was iced with sugar and egg white.

INGREDIENTS

For the flan case

1 quantity pâte brisée pastry (see page 54)

For the filling

60g (2oz) cornflour

150g (5oz) caster sugar

125ml (4fl oz) water

finely grated zest of 1 lemon

125ml (4fl oz) lemon juice

4 egg yolks

30g (1oz) butter

For the topping

4 egg whites

¼ teaspoon of cream of tartar

150g (5oz) caster sugar

1 Allow the pastry to come back to room temperature. Knead briefly on a lightly floured surface, roll out and use to line the prepared flan tin (see page 56). Bake blind in the oven for 10 minutes (see page 56). Uncover and bake for a further

3–4 minutes until gold. Remove from the oven and leave to cool. Lower the oven temperature.

2 For the filling, blend the cornflour, sugar, water, lemon zest and juice in a pan. Slowly bring to the boil, stirring constantly, until thickened and clear. Cook gently for 1 minute.

3 Remove from the heat and beat in the egg yolks, one at a time. Return to the heat and cook gently, stirring, for 1 minute. Remove from the heat, beat in the butter and then spread over the pastry case.

4 For the topping, whisk the egg whites and cream of tartar into soft peaks. Gradually whisk in the sugar to form a stiff, glossy meringue (see page 49). Spread over the pie to make a seal with the pastry edge. Swirl with the tip of a knife and bake for 10 minutes or until golden.

Oven temperature
220°C/425°F/gas 7 for the flan case; 180°C/350°F/gas 4 for the topping

Baking time
14–15 minutes for the flan case; 10 minutes for the topping

Flan tin
23cm (9in) fluted flan tin or non-stick pie plate, greased

Makes
6–8 slices

Storage
Best eaten the day it is made

Step ahead
Make the pastry and chill for 1 hour

Pastries & Biscuits

Homemade pastries and biscuits always add a welcoming note to any invitation for tea or coffee. Here are crisp-baked, toffee-like wafers full of nuts and glacé fruit, light and crunchy sugar biscuits rich in butter, crisp choux puffs filled with fresh berries nestling in softly whipped cream, and wafer-thin almond biscuits shaped like curved roof tiles. These delectable mouthfuls of sweet refreshment are always appreciated and hard to resist, so be sure to make plenty, and if any are left over, store them in an airtight tin.

A SELECTION OF
Butter Biscuits,
Florentines and
Bienenstich

Florentines

Florentines are a luxurious version of the old-fashioned brandy snap. Crisp and lacy, they can be coated with melted chocolate – plain, milk or white. Mark the chocolate lightly with a fork if you want them to look a little more fancy (see page 146). Bake no more than five at a time and watch them carefully as they can burn very easily.

INGREDIENTS

90g (3oz) flaked almonds

30g (1oz) unblanched almonds, coarsely chopped

45g (1½ oz) candied orange and lemon peel, finely chopped

30g (1oz) glacé cherries, washed, dried and cut into small pieces

15g (½ oz) angelica, washed, dried and cut into small pieces

1 tbsp plain flour

100g (3½ oz) butter

100g (3½ oz) granulated sugar

2 tbsp clear honey

2 tbsp double cream

200g (7oz) chocolate, melted (see page 44) to decorate

1 Mix together the flaked and chopped almonds, peel, glacé cherries, angelica and flour.

2 Put the butter, sugar, honey and cream into a pan. Heat gently to dissolve the sugar. Bring to the boil and cook to 120°C/250°F.

3 Stir in the fruit and nut mixture and cook, stirring, for 1 minute until the mixture rolls off the sides of the pan. Remove from the heat.

4 Drop 5 heaped teaspoons of the mixture 7cm (3in) apart on the prepared baking sheet and flatten slightly with a spoon. Bake in the preheated oven for 6–7 minutes until golden.

5 Remove from the oven and quickly reshape by drawing up the mixture inside a 5cm (2in) biscuit cutter. Leave to cool and then transfer to a wire rack. Repeat the process to make about 35 biscuits. Spread the back of each one with chocolate (see page 146) and leave to set.

Oven temperature
180°C/350°F/gas 4

Baking time
6–7 minutes

Cake tin
Flat baking sheet, lined with silicone paper

Makes
35 biscuits

Storage
Keep for 1–2 weeks

Bienenstich

A particular family favourite, these delicious buttery fingers are covered with an almond toffee topping. The fresher they are, the better they taste.

INGREDIENTS

For the topping

100g (3½ oz) butter

100g (3½ oz) caster sugar

2 tbsp light soft brown sugar

2 tbsp milk

250g (8oz) flaked almonds

For the base

125g (4oz) unsalted butter

125g (4oz) caster sugar

1 egg

1 tsp finely grated lemon zest

200g (7oz) plain flour, sifted

1 tsp baking powder

1 For the topping, melt the butter in a medium-sized pan. Stir in the caster and soft brown sugar and the milk. Bring to a rapid boil, stirring all the time, then remove from the heat and stir in the flaked almonds, making sure that all the nuts are well coated with the toffee mixture. Set aside to cool slightly.

2 For the base, beat the butter and sugar together until pale and fluffy. Beat in the egg and lemon zest. Sift the flour and baking powder together. Gradually beat into the butter mixture until evenly mixed.

3 Spread the base mixture evenly into the prepared tin and lightly level the surface. Spoon over the almond topping and spread it out carefully.

4 Bake in the preheated oven for 35 minutes or until golden. Remove from the oven and immediately cut into slices before the topping hardens. Leave in the tin until cold. Remove from the tin and peel off the lining paper.

Oven temperature
180°C/350°F/gas 4

Baking time
35 minutes

Cake tin
23cm (9in) shallow, square tin, greased and base-lined

Makes
15 slices

Storage
Keep for 4–5 days

Butter Biscuits

These piped biscuits are crisp on the outside and slightly soft in the centre. Dip in melted chocolate once they are cool.

INGREDIENTS

125g (4oz) butter

125g (4oz) icing sugar

2 small eggs (size 4), lightly beaten

1 tsp finely grated lemon zest

60g (2oz) ground almonds or hazelnuts

200g (7oz) plain flour, sifted

200g (7oz) plain, milk or white chocolate, melted (see page 44) to decorate

1 Beat the butter and icing sugar together until pale and fluffy. Beat in the eggs and lemon zest. Stir in alternating spoonfuls of the ground nuts and flour until evenly mixed. Cover and chill for 30 minutes.

2 Spoon some mixture into a large piping bag fitted with a 1cm (½in) star-shaped nozzle. Pipe S-shapes, rings or long sticks about 2.5cm (1in) apart on to the prepared baking sheets. Chill for 30 minutes.

3 Bake in the preheated oven for 10 minutes or until golden. Cool on the trays. Dip the biscuits into the melted chocolate and leave to set on silicone paper.

 Oven temperature
190°C/375°F/gas 5

 Baking time
10 minutes

 Cake tins
Two flat baking sheets, greased

 Makes
24 biscuits

 Storage
Keep for 4–5 days

❄ **Freezing**
Freeze for 1–2 months, undecorated

Sugar Biscuits

When I was a child my mother used to make a tinful of these favourite biscuits regularly. My sister and I loved to help her cut out the shapes and then finish them with egg and sugar. (See page 25 for illustration.)

INGREDIENTS

250g (8oz) plain flour, sifted

250g (8oz) chilled butter, cut into pieces

125g (4oz) caster sugar

1 tsp finely grated lemon zest

2 eggs, lightly beaten

granulated, demerara and coloured sugar crystals to decorate

1 Rub together the flour and butter into a fine crumb-like mixture. Stir in the caster sugar, lemon zest and half the beaten egg. Knead briefly on a surface lightly dusted with flour until smooth. Wrap in clingfilm and chill for 30 minutes.

2 Roll out thinly on a lightly floured surface. Cut into shapes using 5cm (2in) cutters, kneading and re-rolling until you have about 60 biscuits.

3 Space 1cm (½in) apart on the prepared baking sheets, brush with the remaining egg and sprinkle the centres with sugar. Bake in the preheated oven for 10–12 minutes until golden. Cool on a wire rack.

 Oven temperature
190°C/375°F/gas 5

 Baking time
10–12 minutes

 Cake tins
Two or three flat baking sheets, greased

 Makes
60 biscuits

 Storage
Keep for 2 weeks

Tuiles

A tuile is a wafer-thin biscuit shaped like a traditional curved French roof tile. When baked, the soft toffee-like pastry needs to be quickly shaped and then left until crisp, so do not try to make more than five at a time. (See page 25 for illustration.)

INGREDIENTS

60g (2oz) ground almonds

75g (2½oz) flaked almonds plus 2 tbsp

60g (2oz) caster sugar

1 tbsp plain flour, sifted

1 egg white, lightly beaten

30g (1oz) butter, melted and cooled

1 tsp dark rum

1 Put the ground almonds, 75g (2½oz) flaked almonds, sugar and flour into a bowl. Stir in the egg white, butter and rum. Cover and chill for 2–3 hours.

2 Drop 5 heaped teaspoons of the mixture, 12cm (5in) apart, on to the prepared baking sheet. Flatten each to 2.5mm (⅛in) thick, sprinkle with the remaining flaked almonds and bake in the preheated oven for 6–8 minutes or until just golden.

3 Remove from the oven, scoop up with a palette knife and press over a rolling pin. Leave for 2–3 minutes to set, then transfer to a wire rack and leave to cool. Repeat with the remaining mixture.

Oven temperature
160°C/325°F/gas 3

Baking time
6–8 minutes

 Cake tin
Flat baking sheet, greased

Makes
15 biscuits

 Storage
Keep for 1 week

Fruit & Cream Puffs

These light and airy choux puffs make a lovely tea-time treat or summertime dessert. The raw, piped choux mixture can be made a few days ahead of time and frozen, then baked directly from the freezer for five minutes longer than normal.

INGREDIENTS

For the pastry

1 quantity choux pastry (see page 57)

For the filling and decoration

300ml (½ pint) double cream

2 tbsp caster sugar

250g (8oz) fresh fruit such as raspberries, blueberries and sliced kiwi fruit

icing sugar

1 Make the choux pastry (see page 57) and spoon into a piping bag fitted with a 1cm (½in) star nozzle.

2 Pipe the mixture into twelve 7.5cm (3in) mounds on to the prepared baking sheet. Carefully brush with the beaten egg left over from making the pastry. Bake in the preheated oven for 25 minutes or until crisp and golden.

3 Remove from the oven and pierce a small hole in the base of each puff with a fine metal skewer. Return to the oven, upside down, for 5 minutes to dry out. Remove from the oven and leave to cool on a wire rack.

4 Slice each puff horizontally in half. For the filling, whip the cream and sugar into soft peaks. Spoon into a piping bag fitted with a 1cm (½in) star nozzle and pipe generously into the bottom of each puff.

5 Arrange a few berries or pieces of kiwi fruit on top of the cream and then cover each puff with its top. Dust with icing sugar to decorate.

 Oven temperature
220°C/425°F/gas 7

 Baking time
30 minutes

 Cake tin
Flat baking sheet, lightly greased, run under cold water and left slightly wet

 Makes
12 puffs

 Storage
Best eaten as soon as they are made

Chocolate Éclairs

A mouthwatering combination of crisp pastry, rich crème pâtissière and dark melted chocolate.

INGREDIENTS

For the pastry

1 quantity choux pastry (see page 57)

For the filling and decoration

90ml (3fl oz) double cream

1 quantity crème pâtissière (see page 151)

125g (4oz) plain chocolate

1 Make the choux pastry (see page 57) and spoon into a piping bag fitted with a 1cm (½in) plain nozzle. Pipe twelve 10cm (4in) lines of pastry 5cm (2in) apart on to the prepared baking sheet. Carefully brush with the beaten egg left over from making the pastry.

2 Bake in the preheated oven for 20 minutes or until crisp and golden. Remove from the oven and pierce a small hole in the base of each one with a fine metal skewer. Return to the oven, upside down, for 3–5 minutes to dry out. Remove from the oven and leave to cool on a wire rack.

3 Slice each éclair horizontally in half. For the filling, whip the cream into stiff peaks then fold it into the crème pâtissière until evenly mixed. Spoon into a piping bag fitted with a 1cm (½in) star nozzle. Pipe into the base of each éclair and then cover with the top.

4 Melt the chocolate (see page 44). Leave to cool slightly, until thickened but not set. Carefully dip the top of each éclair into the melted chocolate or spread the top of each one with chocolate using a small palette knife. Leave, chocolate-side up, on a wire rack to set.

VARIATION

Dip the tops of the éclairs in 1 quantity of vanilla, coffee or chocolate glacé icing (see page 152) instead of the melted chocolate. Leave to set.

 Oven temperature
220°C/425°F/gas 7

 Baking time
23–25 minutes

 Cake tin
Flat baking sheet, lightly greased, run under cold water and left slightly wet

 Makes
12 éclairs

 Storage
Best eaten as soon as they are made

 Step ahead
Make the crème pâtissière

Wedding Cakes

Many of the customs surrounding a wedding ceremony, the feast and the cake are a symbol of sharing between the bride and groom and their guests. In Roman times the cake was simply made of flour, water or wine, and honey, but by the 18th century it had become a multi-layered extravaganza, with great importance being given to the elaborate decoration made of sugarpaste, marzipan and spun sugar depicting architectural and sculptural themes.

Croquembouche

This French confection is made of ingredients that crunch and crumble in the mouth, hence the name "croque-em-bouche". In earlier times, small cakes, fruit or pieces of sugarwork were stuck together with sugar syrup inside a plain, moulded container. When the containers were briefly heated and turned over, the cake would drop out. The familiar choux pastry pyramid is a recent innovation and is the most popular celebration cake in France today.

INGREDIENTS

For the paper cone

one 62.5x50cm (25x20in) sheet of lightweight white card

For the pastry base

1½ quantities pâte brisée pastry (see page 54)

For the choux puffs

4 quantities choux pastry (see page 57)

For the filling

2.5 litres (4 pints) double cream

125–180g (4–6oz) caster sugar

125–175ml (4–6fl oz) brandy

For the caramel glaze

1kg (2lb) granulated sugar

300ml (½ pint) water

cream of tartar

For the decoration

selection of fresh white and lilac flowers

TO MAKE THE CONE

1 Lay the card flat, long-side facing you. Make a mark half way along the top long edge. Draw diagonal lines from this point down to the two bottom corners. Fold along these lines to create a large triangle.

2 Fold this triangle in half, leaving the excess card inside for strength. Measure 50cm (20in) from the narrowest point down each long side and make a mark. Draw a gentle curve from one mark to the other. Cut carefully along the line. This gives a level base to help the cone stand upright.

3 Bend the card into a cone so that the two long edges meet. Stick together with plenty of adhesive tape. Push some foil or tissue paper inside the cone for extra stability. The finished cone should measure 50cm (20in) in height with the base 20cm (8in) in diameter.

TO MAKE THE CAKE

1 For the base, allow the pastry to come back to room temperature. Knead briefly until smooth and roll out on a lightly floured surface into a 30cm (12in) circle.

2 Transfer the pastry to the greased baking sheet and crimp the edge between your fingers. Prick all over with a fork and bake in the preheated oven for 15–20 minutes. Remove from the oven and leave to cool. Lower the oven temperature.

3 For the choux puffs, make the choux pastry (see page 57), one batch at a time. Spoon the first batch into a piping bag fitted with a 1cm (½in) plain nozzle. Pipe the mixture on to the wet baking sheets, in small 1cm (½in) mounds.

4 Bake in the preheated oven for about 15 minutes or until crisp and golden. Pierce a small hole in the base of each puff with a fine metal skewer. Return to the oven, upside down, for 2–3 minutes to dry

Oven temperature
200°C/400°F/gas 6 for the pastry base; 220°C/425°F/gas 7 for the choux puffs

Baking time
15–20 minutes for the pastry base; 15–20 minutes for the choux puffs

Cake tins
Three flat baking sheets, one lightly greased and the others run under cold water and left slightly wet

Makes
Approximately 50–60 portions

Storage
Keeps for 2 hours once assembled

Freezing
Freeze the piped choux mixture for up to 1 month

Step ahead
Make and pipe the choux paste, freeze raw and bake from frozen for 20–25 minutes; make the pastry and chill for 1 hour; make the cone

out. Remove from the oven and leave to cool on wire racks.

5 Repeat this process with the next three batches of pastry, very gradually enlarging the mounds of paste until they are about 2.5cm (1in) in size. As each batch of pastry is used, freeze, or bake immediately, increasing the baking time a little as the puffs get larger. The largest puffs will take about 20 minutes to cook. You will need about 150 puffs in total.

6 For the filling, whip the cream, sugar and brandy into stiff peaks. Spoon a little at a time into a piping bag fitted with a 5mm (¼in) plain nozzle. Pipe into each choux puff and chill for 1 hour.

TO ASSEMBLE THE CAKE

1 Put the pastry base on a large serving plate or cake board and place the cardboard cone in the centre.

2 For the glaze, make up the caramel in four batches as needed. For each batch, put 250g (8oz) sugar and 75ml (2½fl oz) water into a heavy-based pan. Leave over a low heat until the sugar has completely dissolved. Stir in a small pinch of cream of tartar, increase the heat and bring to the boil without stirring. Boil for about 7 minutes until the syrup reaches 173°C (345°F) and has turned a rich caramel colour (see page 153).

3 Remove the pan from the heat and plunge the base into cold water. Leave in a bowl of very hot water, to prevent the caramel from setting, while you assemble the cake.

4 Starting with the largest choux puffs, spear them one at a time on to a metal skewer or fork. Dip the tops quickly into the caramel, covering them well. Slide off the skewer and position side by side around the

base of the cone. Make sure each one sticks to the next.

5 Quickly position a second row of caramel-dipped puffs on top of the first, before they have time to set. Continue working like this, using the puffs in order of size, and making more caramel as you need it, until the cone is covered. Leave to set.

6 Cut the flower stems down to about 1cm (½in). Starting at the top, tuck them in between the puffs in a sweep. Keep in a cool, dry place. Serve within 2 hours.

Arrange the flowers in a decorative cascade

Stick the choux puffs together with caramel

American Wedding Cake

The forerunner of this wedding cake was a two-tiered version that originated in 17th-century France. Unlike the plainer cakes of earlier times, this one was made with rich ingredients. One tier, the "groom's" cake, was dark and heavily fruited. The lighter "bride's" cake was bedecked with spun sugar ornaments. Now, the cakes are more often carrot and butter cakes, sponges and even cheesecakes. For this wedding cake, make two of each of the almond cake layers and sandwich them together in pairs with buttercream, before stacking one on top of the other and decorating. (See page 26 for illustration.)

INGREDIENTS

For each 30cm (12in) orange and almond cake (bottom tier). Make two.

375g (12oz) unsalted butter, softened
375g (12oz) caster sugar
6 eggs
375g (12oz) self-raising flour
finely grated zest of 1 large orange
1 tsp almond extract
125g (4oz) ground almonds
75ml (2½ fl oz) fresh orange juice

For each 20cm (8in) chocolate and almond cake (middle tier). Make two.

180g (6oz) unsalted butter, softened
180g (6oz) caster sugar
3 eggs, separated
180g (6oz) plain chocolate
2 tsp finely grated orange zest
180g (6oz) self-raising flour, sifted
60g (2oz) ground almonds
1 tbsp fresh orange juice

For each 15cm (6in) chocolate and almond cake (top tier). Make two.

125g (4oz) unsalted butter, softened
125g (4oz) caster sugar
2 eggs, separated
125g (4oz) plain chocolate
1 tsp finely grated orange zest
125g (4oz) self-raising flour, sifted
30g (1oz) ground almonds
2 tsp fresh orange juice

For the buttercream

1.5kg (3lb) unsalted butter, softened
2.5kg (5lb) icing sugar, sifted
150ml (¼ pint) fresh orange juice
orange food-colouring powder

To assemble the cake

one 15cm (6in) thin cake board
one 20cm (8in) thin cake board
one 35cm (14in) thick cake board
1 small nylon piping bag
one 1.25mm (⅟₁₆ in) writing nozzle
one 1cm (⅜ in) ribbon nozzle
12 acrylic cake skewers
fresh orange-coloured flowers
10cm (4in) sphere of florist's foam
2 metres (2¼ yards) wide dark orange ribbon
2 metres (2¼ yards) narrow pale orange ribbon

 Oven temperature
180°C/350°F/gas 4

 Baking time
30–35 minutes for each 30cm (12in) cake layer; 25–30 minutes for each 20cm (8in) cake layer; 20–25 minutes for each 15cm (6in) cake layer

Cake tins
One 30cm (12in), one 20cm (8in) and one 15cm (6in) deep, square tin, greased and lined

 Makes
30cm (12in) cake makes 60 slices; 20cm (8in) cake makes 24 slices; 15cm (6in) cake makes 12 slices

Storage
The assembled cake keeps for up to 3 days, without the flower decoration

 Freezing
The sponge cakes can be frozen for 1 month, undecorated

Step ahead
Make the buttercream and sponge layers up to 4 days in advance

1 For the 30cm (12in) orange and almond cake, beat the butter and sugar together until pale and fluffy. Beat in the eggs, one at a time, adding a little of the flour if the mixture begins to curdle. Stir in the orange zest and almond extract. Mix in the flour, almonds and orange juice.

2 Spread the mixture into the prepared tin and bake in the preheated oven for about 30–35 minutes or until a skewer comes out clean. Remove from the oven and leave to cool in the tin. Turn out, peel off the paper and wrap in foil if not using straight away. Repeat for the second layer.

3 For the 20cm (8in) chocolate and almond cake, beat the butter, sugar and egg yolks together until pale and fluffy. Melt the chocolate (see page 44), cool slightly and then stir in with the orange zest. Stir in the flour, almonds and orange juice.

4 In another bowl, whisk the egg whites into soft peaks. Fold 3 spoonfuls into the main mixture to loosen the texture, then gently fold in the rest. Pour into the prepared tin and bake in the preheated oven for 25–30 minutes or until a skewer comes out clean. Remove from the oven and leave to cool in the tin. Turn out, peel off the paper and wrap in foil. Repeat for the second layer.

5 For the 15cm (6in) chocolate and almond cake, follow the method for the 20cm (8in) cake. Pour into the prepared tin and bake in the preheated oven for 20–25 minutes or until a skewer comes out clean. Repeat.

6 For the buttercream, beat 375g (12oz) butter and 625g (1lb 4oz) icing sugar together until smooth. Beat in up to 2½ tablespoons of the orange juice to give a spreading consistency. Repeat three times. Colour one of the four batches orange using a little of the colouring powder.

7 Sandwich together the cakes in pairs with a little of the plain buttercream. Place each one on the appropriate board. Using a warm, dry palette knife, spread the top and sides of each cake with a thin layer of the plain buttercream.

8 Spoon the orange-coloured buttercream into a piping bag fitted with the writing nozzle (see page 145). Pipe an even number of vertical lines, about 1cm (½in) apart, over the sides of each cake and across the top of the smallest cake. Spoon the plain buttercream, a little at a time, into a piping bag fitted with the ribbon nozzle.

9 Starting at the bottom of each cake, pipe horizontally over each alternate line to give a basket-weave design (see page 145). For the next row up, start with the second vertical line in. On the third row, repeat the first line. Continue over all the cakes.

TO ASSEMBLE THE CAKE

1 Measure the depth of the bottom tier. Cut 8 skewers 2.5cm (1in) longer than this measurement. Push them into the cake, in a square 7.5cm (3in) from the edge. Repeat for the middle tier with the remaining skewers, but insert them 5cm (2in) from the edge.

2 Carefully place the middle tier centrally over the bottom one, so that it rests on the skewers. Position the top tier in the same way. Trim the stalks of the flowers to about 3.5cm (1½in) long and pack them between the tiers. Place smaller flowers around the base of the bottom tier.

3 Slice off the top third of the foam sphere and press in more flowers to cover it closely. Set on top of the cake. Trim the sides of the bottom cake board with the ribbons.

Traditional Wedding Cake

The dark, heavily-fruited "groom's" cake still remains the classic English celebration cake, while the decorative white icing on the outside represents the paler "bride's" cake of old. This wedding cake retains the early custom of light and dark layers; the top tier is a dark Traditional Plumb Cake, a layer to be kept until later, for a christening maybe. The two lighter tiers are made of Baumkuchen, the classic German celebration cake. With its roots in pre-Christian Greece, this "tree" cake was once made by pouring the batter on to a wooden skewer turned by hand on a spit over an open fire. Today, thin layers of the batter are toasted one on top of the other in a tin, so they still resemble the rings of a tree when cut across. It should be served in very thin slices. (See page 27 for illustration.)

INGREDIENTS

For the 15cm (6in) Traditional Plumb Cake (top tier)

60g (2oz) dried cranberries
60g (2oz) muscat raisins
90g (3oz) sultanas
90g (3oz) currants
90g (3oz) dried apricots, finely chopped
90ml (3fl oz) dark rum or brandy
1½ tsp finely grated orange zest
1 tbsp orange juice
150g (5oz) plain flour
1 tsp ground cinnamon
¼ tsp ground allspice
60g (2oz) ground almonds
125g (4oz) butter
125g (4oz) light muscovado sugar
2 large eggs (size 1), lightly beaten

For the 23cm (9in) Baumkuchen (middle tier)

500g (1lb) unsalted butter, softened
seeds from ½ of a vanilla pod
finely grated zest of 1 lemon
500g (1lb) caster sugar
14 eggs, separated
250g (8oz) plain flour
250g (8oz) potato flour or cornflour

For the 30cm (12in) Baumkuchen (bottom tier)

1kg (2lb) unsalted butter, softened
seeds from 1 vanilla pod
finely grated zest of 2 lemons
1kg (2lb) caster sugar
28 eggs, separated
500g (1lb) plain flour
500g (1lb) potato flour or cornflour

For the decoration

2 quantities apricot glaze (see page 149)
6½ quantities marzipan (see page 152) or 3.25kg (6lb 4oz) white marzipan
4kg (8lb) champagne-coloured sugarpaste
large assortment of cream and peach coloured flowers such as spray roses
4 egg whites
500g (1lb) caster sugar

To assemble the cake

one 20cm (8in) thick cake board
one 40cm (16in) thick cake board
one 25cm (10in) thin cake board
5 metres (5½ yards) cream satin ribbon
8 acrylic cake skewers
3 hollow champagne-coloured cake pillars

1 Make the 15cm (6in) Plumb Cake (see page 99 for the method). Spoon the mixture into the prepared tin and bake in the preheated oven for 2 hours, covering with greaseproof paper after 1 hour, or until a skewer comes out clean. Remove from the oven and leave to cool. Turn out, peel off the lining paper and wrap in foil.

2 For the 23cm (9in) Baumkuchen, make the cake in two layers, using one 7-egg mixture for each layer. Beat 250g (8oz) butter, half the vanilla, half the lemon zest and 250g (8oz) sugar together until pale and fluffy. Beat in 7 egg yolks, one at a time. Sift together 125g (4oz) each of plain flour and potato flour. Gradually beat in until well combined. In another bowl, whisk the egg whites into soft peaks. Stir in 2 large spoonfuls, then carefully fold in the rest.

3 Preheat the grill to high. Spread 6 tablespoons of the mixture evenly over the base of the smaller prepared tin. Grill for 2–3 minutes until golden and cooked through. Remove, cover with another layer of mixture and grill for 2–3 minutes. After 3–4 layers, you will be able to spread the mixture more thinly. Continue, using about 4 tablespoons of mixture for each layer. Remove the cake from the tin and leave to cool on a wire rack. Repeat to make the second layer.

4 For the two 30cm (12in) Baumkuchen layers, make up the mixture, one 7-egg batch at a time (see step 2). Spread

Oven temperature
150°C/300°F/gas 2 for the 15cm (6in) fruit cake

Baking time
2 hours for the 15cm (6in) fruit cake; about 1 hour grilling time for each 23cm (9in) Baumkuchen layer; about 2 hours grilling time for each 30cm (12in) Baumkuchen layer

Cake tins
One 15cm (6in) deep, round tin for the fruit cake, greased and lined; one 23cm (9in) springform tin and one 30cm (12in) springform tin, bases greased with butter and floured for the Baumkuchen

Makes
15cm (6in) cake makes 20 slices; 23cm (9in) cake makes 40 slices; 30cm (12in) cake makes 70 slices

Storage
15cm (6in) fruit cake will keep for several months in an airtight tin; the Baumkuchen will keep fresh for 3–4 weeks, wrapped in clingfilm and foil; the assembled cake will keep for up to 1 week without the flower decoration

Freezing
The fruit cake will freeze for 1 year

about 10 tablespoons of mixture over the base of the larger prepared tin and grill for 2–3 minutes. After 3–4 layers, reduce to 6–7 tablespoons of mixture. Continue as for the smaller cake, using two 7-egg batches for each layer.

5 Sandwich the two 23cm (9in) Baumkuchen layers together with 2 tablespoons of apricot glaze and the 30cm (12in) layers together with 3–4 tablespoons of glaze. Brush the 15cm (6in) fruit cake with 1–2 tablespoons of glaze. Cover with 375g (12oz) marzipan (see page 140). Brush the 23cm (9in) Baumkuchen with 3–4 tablespoons of glaze and cover with 1kg (2lb) marzipan. Brush the 30cm (12in) Baumkuchen with 5–6 tablespoons of glaze and cover with 1.75kg (3lb 8oz) marzipan.

6 Cover the 20cm (8in) thick cake board with 250g (8oz) sugarpaste and the 40cm (16in) thick board with 500g (1lb) sugarpaste (see page 141). Leave to dry for at least 24 hours. Moisten the marzipan surface of each cake (see page 140). Cover the fruit cake in 500g (1lb) sugarpaste, the 23cm (9in) Baumkuchen in 1kg (2lb)

sugarpaste and the 30cm (12in) Baumkuchen in 1.75kg (3lb 8oz) sugarpaste (see page 141). Place the 23cm (9in) cake on the thin board and trim the thick boards with ribbon.

TO ASSEMBLE THE CAKE
1 Place the 15cm (6in) and the 30cm (12in) cakes on the thick boards. Measure the depth of the 30cm (12in) cake and cut 5 skewers to the same length. Push into the cake, in an evenly spaced circle, about 7cm (3in) from the edge. Measure the depth of the 23cm (9in) cake and the height of the cake pillars and cut the remaining skewers to the length of their combined measurements.

2 Push the skewers into the 23cm (9in) cake in an evenly spaced circle, about 7cm (3in) in from the edge. Position the cake centrally on top of the 30cm (12in) cake. Slide the cake pillars over the skewers and rest the small cake on top. Attach ribbon around the base of each cake. Sugar-frost the flowers using the egg white and caster sugar (see page 148) and leave to dry. Arrange on the cake no more than 6 hours before serving.

Festival Cakes

Preparing a cake for a special occasion, whether religious or secular, has long been a ritual, which has resulted in many rich and luxurious recipes being passed from generation to generation. Indeed, the tradition of baking has its origins in the feasts and festivals of the distant past, and spices, dried fruit and nuts, which were once coveted and costly ingredients, were reserved especially for such times.

THE CAKE'S TEXTURE is dense and honey-enriched, studded with nuts and dried fruit and lightly marbled with chocolate.

Certosino

Special Ingredients

Sultanas can be plumped up in hot water for 30 minutes before using.

Dark rum imparts rich, sweet moisture.

Honey with a fine aroma and clear tones makes the best sweetener.

Cinnamon adds an intense aromatic taste.

Aniseed gives the cake its distinctive liquorice flavour.

Apple purée adds a moist, rich texture.

Almonds are blanched in boiling water, then sliced into thin flakes.

Plain chocolate must be high in cocoa fat for a good flavour.

Pine nuts have a mild but delicious resinous flavour.

Candied fruit, walnuts and pecan nuts are traditional festive decorations.

Making the Cake

This is a traditional Italian Christmas cake that originated with the Carthusian monks of Bologna during medieval times. It is decorated with a sumptuous assortment of nuts and candied fruit.

INGREDIENTS

For the cake

75g (2½ oz) sultanas

1½ tbsp dark rum

350g (12oz) clear honey

45g (1½ oz) butter

3 tbsp water

2 tsp aniseed

400g (13oz) plain flour

1½ tsp bicarbonate of soda

1 tsp ground cinnamon

180g (6oz) apple purée (see page 149)

180g (6oz) blanched almonds, coarsely chopped or flaked

75g (2½ oz) plain chocolate, coarsely chopped

180g (6oz) candied orange and lemon peel, finely chopped

45g (1½ oz) pine nuts

For the decoration

3 tbsp apricot glaze (see page 149)

750g–1kg (1½–2lb) candied fruit, candied peel, walnut or pecan halves

1 For the cake, put the sultanas and rum in a small bowl. Cover with clingfilm and leave to soak for 30 minutes.

2 Put the honey, butter and water together into a heavy-based pan. Set over a low heat and leave until melted. Stir in the aniseed.

3 Sift the flour, bicarbonate of soda and cinnamon into a large bowl. Slowly pour in the honey mixture and mix until smooth. Stir in the apple purée, almonds, chocolate, candied peel, rum-soaked sultanas and pine nuts.

4 Spoon the mixture into the prepared tin and bake in the preheated oven for 1 hour– 1 hour 10 minutes. Remove from the oven and turn out on to a wire rack. Peel off the lining paper and leave to cool.

5 To decorate, brush the top of the cake with half the apricot glaze. Arrange the candied fruit, candied peel and nuts decoratively over the cake and then brush once more with the remaining glaze. Leave to set before serving or storing.

Oven temperature
160°C/325°F/gas 3

Baking time
1 hour–1 hour 10 minutes

Cake tin
23cm (9in) springform tin, greased and base-lined

Makes
16 slices

Storage
Keeps for 1 week

Step ahead
Make the apple purée; soak the sultanas

Pumpkin Pie for Thanksgiving

In the northern hemisphere, pumpkins ripen towards the end of October, just in time for Hallowe'en. In America this pie makes a fitting end to the traditional Thanksgiving feast that falls in late November. Serve with whipped cream on the side.

INGREDIENTS

For the flan case

1 quantity pâte sucrée pastry (see page 55)

For the filling

500ml (16fl oz) pumpkin purée (see page 149)

100g (3½ oz) caster sugar

4 eggs

175ml (6fl oz) double cream

1 tsp ground cinnamon

pinch of ground cloves

pinch of ground mace

2 tbsp sherry, dark rum or Cognac

60g (2oz) stem ginger, drained and finely chopped

1 Allow the pastry to come back to room temperature.

Knead briefly until smooth, roll out on a lightly floured surface and use to line the prepared tin (see page 56). Prick all over with a fork and bake blind (see page 56) in the preheated oven for 20 minutes. Remove from the oven, uncover and leave to cool. Lower the oven temperature.

2 For the filling, beat the pumpkin purée, sugar and eggs together. Stir in the double cream, ground spices and sherry, rum or Cognac and stem ginger.

3 Pour the mixture into the flan case and bake in the oven for 40 minutes or until the filling is set. Remove from the tin and cool slightly before serving.

Oven temperature
200°C/400°F/gas 6 for the flan case; 190°C/375°F/gas 5 for the filling

Baking time
20 minutes for the flan case; 40 minutes for the filling

Flan tin
22cm (8½in) fluted flan tin, greased

Makes
8 slices

Storage
Keeps for 1–2 days

Step ahead
Make the pastry

Bûche de Noël

It is difficult to trace the earliest date of this very popular, traditional French Christmas cake, but an early 20th-century pastry book gives a long and complicated description using a Genoese sponge roulade as a base. The log is decorated to look like a fallen tree covered with lichen and wood shavings, and sprouting with small fungi.

INGREDIENTS

For the cake

1 quantity Biscuit de Savoie sponge mixture (see page 65)

For the filling

450ml (¾ pint) double cream

60g (2oz) caster sugar

1 tbsp Grand Marnier (optional)

1 tbsp finely grated orange zest

For the decoration

1½ quantities chocolate ganache (see page 151)

1–2 tbsp chopped blanched pistachio nuts

1–2 tbsp toasted flaked almonds

1 quantity meringue mushrooms (see page 148)

cocoa powder and icing sugar

1 Make the Biscuit de Savoie sponge mixture (see page 65). Pour into the prepared tins and bake in the preheated oven for 10 minutes, swapping the trays from one shelf to the other after 5 minutes.

2 Remove from the oven, cover with clean silicone paper and slightly damp tea towels and leave to cool. For the filling,

whip the cream, caster sugar, Grand Marnier and orange zest together into stiff peaks.

3 Uncover the sponges and turn out on to silicone paper sprinkled with caster sugar. Peel off the lining paper, trim the edges and spread over the cream. Starting with one short edge, roll up (see page 53). Cut a thin slice off each end of one roll. Cut the second roll in half.

TO FINISH THE CAKE

1 Lay the whole cake and one half end to end and seam-side down on a serving plate. Diagonally cut one third off the remaining piece of cake. Position the larger piece at an angle on one side of the log, and the smaller piece, cut side up, on top. Spread the ganache over the top and sides of the log. Chill for 1 hour.

2 Decorate the chocolate log with the chopped pistachio nuts and meringue mushrooms. Dust with a little cocoa powder and icing sugar.

Oven temperature
230°C/450°F/gas 8

Baking time
10 minutes

Cake tins
Two 24x33.5x1cm (9½ x13½ x½ in) Swiss roll tins, greased and lined

Makes
20–24 slices

Storage
Keeps for 3–4 days

Freezing
Freezes for 1 month, undecorated

Step ahead
Make the meringue mushrooms

Paskha

*U*nlike the traditional festive yeasted fruit breads of *Russia*, Paskha *is a fruited and spiced cheesecake. It was traditionally pressed into a wooden pyramid-shaped mould carved with an Orthodox cross. (See page 17 for illustration.)*

INGREDIENTS

250g (8oz) unsalted butter, softened

180g (6oz) caster sugar

500g (1lb) curd cheese

2 egg yolks

125ml (4fl oz) double cream

3 drops vanilla extract

125g (4oz) raisins

60g (2oz) candied orange and lemon peel, finely chopped

2 tbsp chopped blanched pistachio nuts

125g (4oz) toasted blanched almonds, chopped

250g (8oz) candied clementines, citron, pears, melon and orange peel to decorate

1 Beat the butter and sugar together until pale and fluffy. Beat in the curd cheese until smooth, followed by the egg yolks, one at a time. Stir in the double cream and vanilla extract. Add the raisins, candied peel, chopped pistachio nuts and almonds. Stir gently until everything is evenly mixed.

2 Spoon the mixture into the prepared mould and press down lightly. Lift the excess cloth over the top of the filling and tuck in around the edge. Lay a small plate inside the rim so that it sits on the mixture and place a heavy weight on top. Set the mould on a plate and chill for 6 hours or overnight.

3 Shortly before serving, invert the Paskha on to a plate. Carefully lift off the pot, then the muslin. Thinly slice the candied clementines and citron peel and arrange around the base of the Paskha. Cut the remaining fruit into small diamonds and arrange in four crosses on opposite sides of the Paskha, together with a smaller one on top. Serve in thin slices.

 Cake mould
Flowerpot, 15cm (6in) across the top and 14cm (5½ in) high, lined with a large piece of damp muslin

 Makes
10–12 slices

 Storage
Keeps for 2–3 days

Warning
This recipe contains raw eggs (see page 9)

Swiss Carnival Wafers

*T*hese crisp, disc-shaped delicacies are deep-fried in oil and then heavily dusted with icing sugar. Use an oil with an indistinct flavour for cooking, such as corn, sunflower or groundnut oil.

INGREDIENTS

2 eggs

30g (1oz) caster sugar

60ml (2fl oz) extra thick double cream

250g (8oz) plain flour, sifted

pinch of salt

finely grated zest of 1 lemon

2 tbsp vanilla sugar

oil for deep-frying

3 tbsp icing sugar to decorate

1 Beat the eggs and sugar together well until thick, pale and creamy. Gradually beat in the cream.

2 Sift together the flour and the salt. Gently fold half into the egg mixture with the lemon zest and vanilla sugar.

3 Add the remaining flour and mix into a soft dough. If the mixture is still sticky, mix in a little extra flour. Knead briefly on a lightly floured surface until smooth. Wrap in clingfilm and chill for 1–2 hours.

4 Divide the mixture equally into 20 pieces. Shape each piece into a ball and then roll out on a lightly floured work surface into wafer-thin discs about 12cm (5in) in diameter. Brush off any surplus flour.

5 Heat the oil in a large, deep pan to 180°C (350°F) or until a cube of bread browns and rises to the top in 1 minute.

6 Drop the discs one at a time into the hot oil and cook for 12–15 seconds or until puffed up, crisp and golden. Turn and fry for another 5 seconds. Lift out with a slotted spoon and leave to drain on a wire rack covered with kitchen paper. Dust heavily with the icing sugar when cold.

 Makes
20 wafers

 Storage
Keep for at least 2 weeks

Swedish Saffron Plait for Sankta Lucia

In celebration of Sankta Lucia, the Swedish festival of light that falls on December 13th, the youngest girl in a family wears a long white gown and a crown of lingonberry leaves ringed with candles. She awakens her parents very early in the morning and offers them a tray set with coffee and freshly baked saffron buns. This is a similar dough, shaped into a plaited loaf.

INGREDIENTS

250ml (8fl oz) milk
90g (3oz) butter
½ tsp saffron
500g (1lb) strong plain flour
two 6g sachets easy-blend dried yeast
125g (4oz) caster sugar
pinch of salt
1 egg yolk
90g (3oz) raisins
90g (3oz) chopped mixed peel
60g (2oz) blanched almonds, finely chopped

For the decoration

1 egg, lightly beaten
1 tbsp chopped blanched almonds
1 tbsp preserving sugar crystals

1 Heat the milk and butter in a small pan until the butter has melted. Stir in the saffron and leave to cool slightly.

2 Sift the flour, yeast, sugar and salt together into a large bowl. Make a well in the centre and add the buttery milk and the egg yolk. Gradually mix the flour into the liquid ingredients, adding a little more flour if the mixture is too wet, until it forms a ball of soft dough.

3 Knead the dough on a lightly floured surface for 10 minutes until smooth and elastic. Place in a large, clean bowl, cover with clingfilm and leave in a warm place for 1½ hours or until doubled in size.

4 Turn out the dough and knead for 5 minutes more. Knead in the raisins, mixed peel and almonds. Cut into three even-sized pieces.

TO SHAPE THE PLAIT

1 Knead each piece of dough into a ball and then roll each one into a 35cm (14in) long rope. Lightly plait the three pieces together and tuck the loose ends underneath.

2 Transfer the plait to the prepared baking sheet, cover with a dry cloth and leave in a warm place for 45 minutes or until doubled in size.

3 Uncover the plait and brush with the egg. Sprinkle over the almonds and sugar and bake in the preheated oven for 30–40 minutes. Cover with foil during baking if it starts to over-brown. Leave to cool on a wire rack.

 Oven temperature
200°C/400°F/gas 6

 Baking time
30 minutes

 Cake tin
Flat baking sheet, greased

 Makes
18 slices

 Storage
Keeps for 1 week

 Freezing
Freezes for 2 months

Italian Easter Cake

Here is an unusual Easter cake from Naples that uses two traditional Italian ingredients: ricotta cheese and vermicelli pasta, which are baked in a sweet "pasta frolla" shortcrust pastry case.

INGREDIENTS

For the pasta frolla pastry

180g (6oz) plain flour
pinch of salt
125g (4oz) butter, cut into pieces
100g (3½oz) caster sugar
3 egg yolks, lightly beaten
1 tsp finely grated lemon zest

For the filling

350ml (12fl oz) milk
60g (2oz) vermicelli pasta, broken into small pieces
pinch of salt
¼ tsp ground cinnamon
100g (3½oz) caster sugar plus 3 tbsp
375g (12oz) ricotta or curd cheese
3 eggs, separated
60g (2oz) candied orange and lemon peel, finely chopped
1½ tbsp lemon juice
½ tsp finely grated lemon zest
3 tbsp dark rum
icing sugar to decorate

1 For the pastry, sift the flour and salt into a bowl. Make a well in the centre, add the butter, sugar, egg yolks and lemon zest and gradually mix together with a round-bladed knife until everything starts to stick together. Knead gently on a lightly floured surface until smooth. Wrap in clingfilm and chill for 30 minutes.

2 For the filling, bring the milk to the boil. Add the vermicelli, salt, a pinch of the cinnamon and 1 tablespoon of sugar. Simmer, uncovered, for 15–20 minutes, stirring now and then, until all the liquid has been absorbed. Leave to cool.

3 Beat together the cheese and 100g (3½oz) of sugar until smooth. Beat in the egg yolks and vermicelli, followed by the remaining cinnamon, candied peels, lemon juice, zest and rum.

4 In another bowl, whisk 2 egg whites into soft peaks. Whisk in the remaining sugar. Gently fold into the cheese mixture.

5 Set aside one third of the pastry. Roll out the remainder on a lightly floured surface into a 30cm (12in) circle and use to line the prepared tin. Pour in the filling. Use the rest of the pastry for the lattice top (see below). Seal the strips on to the pastry edge, then trim.

6 Brush with the remaining egg white. Place in the preheated oven, lower the oven temperature and bake for 1 hour or until set and golden. Remove and leave to cool on a wire rack. Take out of the tin and dust with icing sugar before serving.

 Oven temperature
200°C/400°F/gas 6, then 180°C/350°F/gas 4

 Baking time
1 hour

 Cake tin
23cm (9in) springform tin, lightly greased

 Makes
10 slices

Storage
Best eaten the day it is made

Making a Pastry Lattice

1 *Roll out the pastry on a lightly floured surface and cut into twelve 1cm (½in) wide strips using a pastry wheel or a knife.*

2 *Lay six of the strips, side by side, about 2.5cm (1in) apart, over the top of the cake, leaving the edges overhanging.*

3 *Lay the remaining strips across at right angles to the first, weaving them under and over to make a lattice pattern.*

Lightly dust the top of the cake with icing sugar before serving.

Children's Party Cakes

"And they saw that the little house was built of bread, and covered with little cakes; but the windows were made of pale sugar." In the 19th century, German bakers, inspired by this fairy-tale house from *Hansel and Gretel*, created a cake made of spiced dough, covered with white icing, bonbons and chocolate. The magic remains today in children's birthday cakes that are brightly coloured and decorated with sweets and chocolates.

Little Houses

A Christmas fair is held each year in Nürnberg, Germany, where festive trinkets, cakes, spicy biscuits and little gingerbread houses are sold. My recipe uses simple sponge cakes cut into small house shapes, covered with sugarpaste and decorated with icing or even favourite sweets. For large numbers of children, you can set several cakes in a row to create a street of houses.

INGREDIENTS

For the cake

½ quantity Victoria Sandwich mixture (see page 66)

For the decoration

4 tbsp apricot glaze (see page 149)

250g (8oz) sugarpaste (see page 152)

food colouring paste

250g (8oz) icing sugar, sifted

1 egg white

chocolate sticks, square chocolate thins, or chocolate buttons for the roofs

1 Make the cake mixture and spoon into the prepared tin. Bake in the preheated oven for 1 hour or until a skewer comes out clean. Turn out on to a wire rack and leave to cool. Peel off the lining paper.

2 Cut the cake crossways into two shorter blocks and separate. Slice off the two corners from each cut end to make the roofs. Trim the other sides flat to give two 7cm (3in) cubes with a roof shape on top. Brush with the apricot glaze.

3 Cut the sugarpaste in half. Knead a very small amount of food colouring into each. On a work surface lightly dusted with icing sugar, roll out each piece into a strip about 7x30cm (3x12in). Wrap neatly around the flat sides of the cubes.

4 Gradually beat the icing sugar into the egg white until smooth. Spoon into a small paper piping bag (see page 144) and snip a tiny piece off the end to make a very small hole. Pipe the door and windows on one side of each cake. Arrange the chocolates over the tops as tiles.

 Oven temperature
160°C/325°F/gas 3

 Baking time
1 hour

 Cake tin
500g (1lb) loaf tin, greased and base-lined

 Makes
2 houses

 Storage
Keep for 1–2 days, undecorated or 3–4 days decorated

 Freezing
Freeze for 1 month, undecorated

 Step ahead
Make the apricot glaze; make and colour the sugarpaste

Hedgehog Cake

This appealing cake is very easy to make. A light and fudgy sponge, made by the all-in-one method, is covered with chocolate icing and decorated with flaked chocolate spines. Make and decorate the cake a couple of days ahead of time to allow the flavours to develop. (See page 29 for illustration.)

INGREDIENTS

For the cake

200g (7oz) self-raising flour
200g (7oz) caster sugar
125g (4oz) butter, softened
2 eggs
2 tbsp drinking chocolate powder
75ml (5 tbsp) evaporated milk
75ml (5 tbsp) water

For the icing and decoration

300ml (½ pint) double cream
100g (3½ oz) plain chocolate, finely grated
10–12 large chocolate flake bars
125g (4oz) walnut or white almond marzipan, coloured light brown with a drop of brown food colouring
1 red candy-coated sweet
2 chocolate dots

1 For the cake, put all the ingredients into a bowl and beat together until light and fluffy. Spoon into the prepared pudding basin, place on a baking tray and bake in the preheated oven for 1 hour or until a skewer inserted into the cake comes out clean. Remove from the oven and leave to rest for 5 minutes. Turn out on to a wire rack and leave to cool.

2 For the icing, bring the cream slowly to the boil. Immediately take off the heat and stir in the grated chocolate. Mix well, leave to cool and then chill for 1–3 hours until very thick and spreadable.

3 Cut each flake bar roughly into four lengthways. Cut each one into small 2.5cm (1in) "spikes". The pieces do not have to be regular or even in shape.

4 Trim the base of the cake level so that it sits flat and place cut-side down on a chopping board. Cut in half vertically. Spread a little of the chocolate icing on to each side of the flat base and press both iced sides together to make the hedgehog's body. Place on a cake board or large plate.

TO FINISH THE CAKE
Mould the marzipan into a small cone-shape for the hedgehog's face. Attach it to one end of the body with a little of the icing. Spread the rest of the icing all over the body. Starting at the back of the hedgehog, push the "spikes" into the icing at a slight angle, saving the smallest pieces for the area at the front around the face. Using a little more icing, attach the red sweet to the tip of the cone for the nose and the chocolate dots for the eyes. Chill for 2 hours to set the icing before serving.

 Oven temperature
180°C/350°F/gas 4

 Baking time
1 hour

 Cake mould
900ml (1½ pint) round-bottomed, glass pudding basin, greased and base-lined with a small circle of silicone paper

 Makes
16 slices

 Storage
Keeps for 3–4 days

 Freezing
Freezes for 1 month, undecorated

Teddy Bear Cake

A cake for teddy bear devotees. Plain and chocolate Genoese sponges, made with half the amount of butter to give a less rich cake, are filled with a layer of jam, shaped into a teddy bear and decorated with brightly coloured sugarpaste. To make a very simple version, just make one 23cm (9in) square sponge and cover with buttercream. Then instead of making a teddy-shaped cake, simply use the template (see page 156) to cut out the various shapes from coloured sugarpaste and place them on the cake.

INGREDIENTS

For the plain cake

90g (3oz) unsalted butter
180g (6oz) caster sugar
6 eggs
180g (6oz) plain flour
1½ tsp finely grated lemon zest

For the chocolate cake

150g (5oz) plain flour
30g (1oz) cocoa powder
90g (3oz) butter
180g (6oz) caster sugar
6 eggs

For the decoration

one thick 28cm (11in) square cake board
1.25kg (2lb 8oz) sugarpaste (see page 152)
1.15 metres (1¼ yards) blue ribbon
90ml (6 tbsp) apricot jam
1 quantity simple buttercream (see page 150)
yellow, blue, red and green food colouring paste
4 tbsp apricot glaze (see page 149)
3 coloured water bomb balloons
3 short pieces fine coloured ribbon

1 Make the plain cake following the method for Rich Genoese Sponge (see page 67). Pour into the prepared tin and bake in the preheated oven for 20–25 minutes or until a skewer comes out clean. Remove from the oven and leave to rest for 5 minutes. Turn out on to a wire rack, peel off the lining paper and leave to cool. For the chocolate cake, sift the flour with the cocoa and follow the same method.

2 Cover the cake board with 250g (8oz) of sugarpaste (see page 141). Trim the edge of the board with the ribbon and leave to dry for 2–3 hours.

3 Cut each cake horizontally in half. Sandwich one plain cake layer between two chocolate layers using the apricot jam. Spread a thin layer of the simple buttercream over the whole cake. On a surface lightly dusted with icing sugar, roll out 500g (1lb) sugarpaste into a 35cm (14in) square and use to cover the cake (see page 141). Position the cake in the middle of the board. Save a small piece of white sugarpaste for the eye.

4 Trace the bear shape and a number on to greaseproof paper (see page 156) and cut out. Use the template to cut the remaining plain cake into a bear shape. Cut the cake trimmings into a variety of small squares to form the presents.

5 Colour 150g (5oz) of the sugarpaste yellow. Divide the rest into three and colour blue, red and green. Brush the bear with apricot glaze. Roll out the yellow sugarpaste and cover the bear. Re-roll the trimmings and cut out the top leg shape and a number using the template. Shape a small piece for the nose and roll the remainder into thin ribbons for the presents.

6 Make the eye from the reserved white and a little blue sugarpaste. Attach the leg, nose, ears and eye with a little water. Mark the fingers and mouth with a skewer.

7 Roll out the blue sugarpaste and cut out the jumper using the template. Roll another piece into a thin rope and use to trim the number. Shape a little red icing into a bow tie and 20 small dots and place on the bear. Use the remaining icing to cover the presents, and use the trimmings for ribbons and bows.

8 Position the bear, a few of the presents and the number on the cake as shown. Give away any remaining presents as party favours. Tie the balloons with the ribbon. Secure to the bear's hand with water and sugarpaste.

 Oven temperature
180°C/350°F/gas 4

 Baking time
20–25 minutes for each cake

 Cake tin
23cm (9in) deep, square tin, greased and lined

 Makes
25 slices

 Storage
Keeps for 1 week

 Freezing
Sponges freeze for 1 month, undecorated

 Step ahead
Make the sugarpaste, cover the cake board and leave to dry for 2–3 hours; make the simple buttercream and apricot glaze

Ribbon & Candle Cake

Some years ago an American friend held a birthday party for her daughter, Elizabeth, in a park. Each child was given a picnic basket filled with a tempting selection of little sandwiches, crisps and fruit. The birthday cake for dessert was a large, moist square of delicious carrot, almond and orange cake covered with cream cheese frosting and colourfully bedecked with candles and ribbons. The children loved it. (See page 28 for illustration.)

INGREDIENTS

For the cake

250g (8oz) plain flour, sifted
2 tsp baking powder
½ tsp bicarbonate of soda
pinch of salt
1½ tsp ground cinnamon
300g (10oz) raw carrots, peeled, finely grated and patted dry with kitchen paper
125g (4oz) ground almonds
250g (8oz) light muscovado sugar
3 eggs
finely grated zest of 1 orange
125g (4oz) butter, melted and cooled

For the decoration

2 quantities cream cheese frosting (see page 150)
one thick 30cm (12in) octagonal cake board
one large sheet pink coloured paper
1.15 metres (1¼ yards) matching pink ribbon for the edge of the board
6 ivory taper candles
2.3 metres (2½ yards) fine pink ribbons
1.15 metres (1¼ yards) wide dark pink ribbon

1 Make the cake following the recipe for the American Carrot Loaf (see page 89 for the method). Pour into the prepared tin and bake in the preheated oven for 30 minutes or until a skewer inserted into the cake comes out clean. Remove from the oven and turn out on to a wire rack. Peel off the lining paper and leave to cool.

2 Cover the cake board with the paper and trim the edge with the ribbon. Cut off each corner of the cake at an angle to make an octagon, so that each of the eight sides measures 10cm (4in). Position the cake on the board. Spread two thirds of the frosting evenly over the top and sides of the cake.

3 Spoon the remaining frosting into a piping bag fitted with a 1cm (½in) star nozzle and pipe in a shell design (see page 145) around the base and top edge of the cake. Chill for 30 minutes.

4 Cut the candles to the desired length. Wrap short pieces of the fine ribbons around the candles and arrange in the centre of the cake. Fix the dark ribbon around the cake.

 Oven temperature
180°C/350°F/gas 4

 Baking time
30 minutes

 Cake tin
23cm (9in) deep, square tin, greased and base-lined

 Makes
18 slices

 Storage
Leave to mature for 2–3 days; keeps for 1–2 days once decorated

 Freezing
Freezes for 1 month, undecorated

 Step ahead
Make the cream cheese frosting; cover the cake board and prepare the candles

4

Icings, Fillings & Decorations

It is the finishing touches that often
make a cake memorable. Here,
clearly illustrated instructions show
how to achieve a professional look,
whether applying the simplest
dusting of icing sugar, sugar-frosting
fresh flowers, or piping a decorative
icing. There are also key recipes for
a selection of buttercreams, icings
and other luxurious finishes and
elegant decorations.

Icings & Other Finishes

A covering of icing can turn a simple cake into a luxurious centrepiece. Cakes for special occasions are often covered in sugarpaste. Rich fruit cakes need a layer of marzipan first.

If the top of the cake is not flat, start by levelling it with a separate circle of marzipan. Sponge cakes can be given a softer finish with glacé icing or buttercream.

COVERING IN MARZIPAN (see page 152, 20cm/8in Round Fruit Cake)

1 Brush the cake with apricot glaze. To level the top, roll out 250g (8oz) marzipan into a circle just larger than the cake's diameter. Invert the cake on to it and press the excess into any gaps.

2 Transfer the cake to a 25cm (10in) round cake board, top-side up. To cover the whole cake with a layer of marzipan, measure across the top and down the sides with a piece of string.

3 Place 750g (1½lb) marzipan on a surface lightly dusted with icing sugar. Roll out with a long, straight-ended rolling pin into a large circle, using the piece of string as a guide.

4 Brush the marzipan top with a little brandy. Using the rolling pin, lift the circle of marzipan over the cake and press smoothly on to the top and sides. Neatly trim off the excess at the base.

5 Leave the surface to dry in a cool, dry place for at least 24 hours. When ready to cover the cake with sugarpaste, brush the marzipan surface with brandy or boiled water once more.

Moistening the marzipan helps sugarpaste to adhere

Brushing with brandy adds rich flavour

COVERING IN SUGARPASTE (see page 152)

1 Measure the depth and diameter of the cake with string as step 2 opposite. Knead the sugarpaste until smooth. Roll out into a circle on a surface dusted with icing sugar, using the string as a guide. Gently lift it over the rolling pin.

2 Carefully lift the sugarpaste. With one edge touching the board nearest to you, drape it over the moistened surface of the cake and let it fall neatly down the other side. Gently smooth it on to the top and sides of the cake.

Lay the sugarpaste over the cake quickly before it stretches out of shape

Rich fruit cakes must be covered in marzipan before icing with sugarpaste

3 Dip your fingers in cornflour or icing sugar and carefully smooth away any creases. For a finer finish, rub the icing lightly with a cake smoother.

4 Neatly trim away the excess icing at the base with a small, sharp knife. Carefully run a palette knife under the cake and lift it off the board.

5 Roll out 250g (8oz) sugarpaste into a circle a little larger than the board. Brush the board with apricot glaze (see page 149). Lay the icing over it and trim.

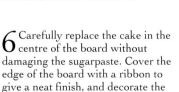

6 Carefully replace the cake in the centre of the board without damaging the sugarpaste. Cover the edge of the board with a ribbon to give a neat finish, and decorate the top of the cake as desired.

HANDY TIP

◆ *Before icing with sugarpaste, cover rich fruit cakes with marzipan to prevent the colour of the cake from staining the icing. Coat sponge cakes with apricot glaze or a little buttercream.*

Icing Sponge Cakes

Choose flavourings that complement the cake: buttercreams enhance rich cakes; plainer cakes can be finished with a simple glacé icing or just a light dusting of icing sugar.

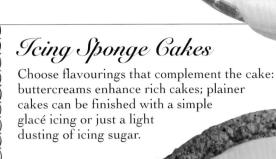

GLACE ICING (see page 152)

1 Place the cake on a wire rack set over a tray or large plate to catch the excess icing. Brush the surface of the cake with apricot glaze if specified in the recipe and leave for 2–3 minutes until set. Pour the icing on to the centre of the cake.

BUTTERCREAM (see page 150)

2 As the icing starts to spread out, coax it gently over the top and down the sides of the cake with a palette knife, so that it coats the whole surface in a smooth, even layer.

3 Leave the icing to set and then carefully transfer the cake to a serving plate. Decorate as desired.

--- *HANDY TIP* ---

• *It is important to get the consistency of glacé icing right. If too liquid, it will run straight off, and if too thick, it will not give a smooth finish.*

1 Place the cake on a wire rack. Make sure the buttercream is at room temperature. Spread it in an even layer over the top of the cake with a palette knife, using a paddling action.

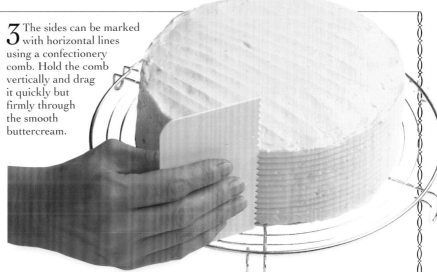

3 The sides can be marked with horizontal lines using a confectionery comb. Hold the comb vertically and drag it quickly but firmly through the smooth buttercream.

2 Spread a layer of buttercream over the sides of the cake using the palette knife. Make sure the layer is generous and even.

FINISHING THE SIDES OF A CAKE

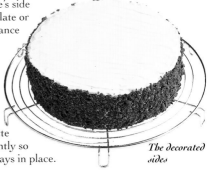

To decorate a cake's side with grated chocolate or chopped nuts, balance the covered cake on the palm of one hand. Hold it over a plate of coating. Lift the coating on to the sides of the cake using a large palette knife, pressing gently so that the coating stays in place.

The decorated sides

GLAZING A FRUIT FLAN

Give cakes and desserts covered in fresh fruit an attractive glossy finish by carefully spooning over a thin, even layer of a jam-based glaze (see page 149), making sure all the fruit is well covered.

DUSTING WITH ICING SUGAR

For a simple finish, place the cold cake on a wire rack and spoon a little icing sugar into a fine-mesh sieve. Hold it about 7cm (3in) above the cake and tap the side, moving it a little each time, to give a light, even dusting.

Piping Methods

A decorative design of piped icing or whipped cream can transform the simplest cake into something quite stunning. For more liquid icings and melted chocolate, it is best to work with small amounts using a homemade paper piping bag. A nylon piping bag fitted with a piping nozzle is better for larger quantities of whipped cream and thicker buttercreams.

MAKING A PAPER PIPING BAG

1 Unroll a length of greaseproof paper. Fold one corner of the paper across to meet the opposite corner of an imaginary square. Crease and cut along the fold to remove a triangle of paper.

2 Fold the triangle in half to make a smaller triangle. Place it on a flat surface with the longest side facing vertically towards you. Bring the top point down to meet the middle one.

3 Fold the paper down twice to meet the bottom point. Open up into a cone. Turn over the edge above the seam to secure (see inset). Snip off the tip, fill and fold over the top to seal.

FILLING A NYLON PIPING BAG

1 Drop a nozzle into the bag, pushing it to the end so no gaps are left. Hold the bag half-way up and fold back the excess fabric. Half fill, pushing the icing or cream down to remove air pockets.

2 Unfold the fabric and tightly twist just above the filling. Hold upright, with one hand firmly holding the twisted top and the other placed more lightly further down to guide the piping.

3 Squeeze from the top of the piping bag with a firm and even pressure, re-twisting the bag as it empties, so that the remaining space always stays full. Refill when necessary.

PIPED DESIGNS

Hold the bag next to, but not quite touching, the surface of the cake as you work. Apply even pressure when piping and always stop squeezing before removing the bag. For most designs you will need a 1cm (½in) star nozzle. For basket-weave, fit one paper piping bag with a 1.25mm (¹⁄₁₆in) plain writing or star nozzle, and a second paper piping bag with a 1cm (½in) ribbon nozzle.

For small stars (see Esterházy Cream Torte, page 71). Hold the bag upright. Squeeze out a small mound of icing without twisting the bag.

For rosettes (see Dobos Torta, page 74). Hold the bag upright. Use a circular motion to form a swirl with a peak.

1cm (½in) star nozzle

For shells (see Mocha Tranche, page 116). Hold the bag at a 95° angle towards you. Pipe briefly away from you, then curl the icing back over and down on itself. Start the next one with the nozzle slightly in front of the tip of the last shell.

For a rope (see Gâteau St Honoré, page 76). Hold the bag at a 95° angle towards you. Pipe in a continuous movement, twisting the icing into a tight spiral.

For basket-weave (see American Wedding Cake, page 124). Pipe vertical lines with the star or writing nozzle, about 1cm (½in) apart, over the surface of the cake. With the ribbon nozzle at the top edge or base of the cake, pipe a short horizontal strip of icing over the outermost vertical line, up to the next line. Continue over every alternate line. Pipe a second strip of horizontal icing alongside the first, starting at the second vertical line in. Repeat to cover.

1cm (½in) ribbon nozzle

1.25mm (¹⁄₁₆in) star nozzle

For chocolate fans (see Orange and Chocolate Layer Cake, page 81). Spoon a little melted chocolate into a paper icing bag. Seal and snip off the tip. Pipe fans on to a baking sheet lined with silicone paper. When set, gently lift off.

Paper icing bag with tip cut off

Decorating with Chocolate

Chocolate gives an elegant finish to all types of cakes and biscuits. It can be melted (see page 44) and used simply as it is, incorporated into more luxurious icings, or made into small, individual decorations. Refrigerate chocolate-covered cakes, biscuits and decorations briefly to help them set, then avoid touching them as chocolate marks very easily and soon melts.

MAKING CHOCOLATE CARAQUE

1 Spread 125g (4oz) melted chocolate on to a scratch-proof surface in a thin, even layer with a palette knife. Leave at room temperature until dry and set.

2 Hold both ends of a large, sharp knife at a 45° angle. Pull it gently across the chocolate's surface so that the chocolate rolls up into long curls.

Chocolate caraque

COATING BISCUITS IN CHOCOLATE

Spread the underside of each biscuit with an even layer of melted chocolate using a small, round-bladed knife. Leave to set very slightly. Mark the chocolate surface with a wavy design using a fork. Leave to set, chocolate-side up, on a rack before serving or storing.

Florentine biscuits

MAKING CHOCOLATE LEAVES

1 Choose non-toxic leaves such as rose, violet or mint. Rinse and dry well before using. With a small, clean paint brush, coat the underside of each leaf with a thin layer of melted chocolate.

2 When the first layer has set, coat once more. Chill in the refrigerator for a few minutes. Carefully peel the leaves away from the chocolate, being careful not to touch it too much.

Chocolate rose leaves

Pour the icing on to the centre of the cake

COVERING A CAKE IN RICH CHOCOLATE ICING

This is the classic icing for Sacher Torte (see page 83), but it can also be used to cover other chocolate and sponge cakes. Leave to set somewhere cool before slicing.

1 Pour 200ml (7fl oz) double cream into a pan, place over a low heat and bring slowly to the boil. Take off the heat, add 150g (5oz) finely grated plain chocolate and stir well until melted. Leave to cool and thicken slightly, stirring now and then. Use while still warm and liquid.

2 Place the cake on a rack over a plate. Pour the icing on to the cake. Tilt the rack until the cake is covered in a smooth, even layer. Leave to set, then transfer to a serving plate. The icing will stay glossy for about 24 hours.

MAKING CHOCOLATE CURLS

Use at room temperature

Bring a bar of chocolate to room temperature. Using a sharp, swivel-bladed vegetable peeler, shave small curls from the sides of the bar.

GRATING CHOCOLATE

Chill the chocolate in the freezer for a short time before using to prevent the chocolate from sticking to the grater. Grate on the largest-sized holes, using a grater or a food processor.

Cake Decorations

It is the attention to small finishing details that gives a cake an attractive, professional appearance. This requires a little extra time and patience, but no particular skill. Some decorations can be prepared in advance, then arranged on the cake when needed. Flowers have a much shorter life, so leave them in plenty of water in a cool place before using and prepare them as near to the time as possible.

FRESH FLOWER DECORATIONS

Simplicity is elegance, and flowers, with their fleeting freshness, transform the plainest cake into an exciting and sumptuous confection. Choose flowers that are safe to use with food, preferably garden-grown and not sprayed with chemicals. Select those with strong stems and thick petals such as roses and rose buds, carnations, violas and pansies, sweet peas, nasturtiums and day lilies.

SUGAR-FROSTED FLOWERS

1 Cut off the flower head, leaving a short stem attached. With a small, clean paint brush, carefully coat each petal as evenly as possible with a thin layer of lightly beaten egg white.

2 Spoon a little caster sugar between each petal, making sure each one is well coated, and then shake out the excess sugar. Carefully push the stems through a wire rack and leave to dry.

MARZIPAN CARROTS

Knead 60g (2oz) white marzipan until smooth. Knead in a little orange food colouring powder until you reach the required shade. Divide the marzipan into 16 even-sized pieces and roll between your fingers into small carrot shapes. Mark each one with ridges using a cocktail stick. Cut a piece of angelica into small strips and push one into the fatter end of each carrot to make a stalk.

FROSTED GRAPES

Separate the grapes from the stalk. Dip one at a time into unbeaten egg white, then spoon over caster sugar to coat evenly. Leave to dry on silicone paper.

MERINGUE MUSHROOMS

1 Whisk 1 egg white into soft peaks. Gradually whisk in 60g (2oz) caster sugar to make a stiff, glossy meringue. Spoon into a piping bag fitted with a 5mm (¼in) plain nozzle.

2 For the caps, pipe twenty 2.5cm (1in) mounds on to a lined baking sheet. Pipe the remainder into twenty small high-peaked stalks. Bake in the oven at 150°C/300°F/gas 2 for ¾ hour. Remove and cool. Make a small hole in the base of each cap with a fine skewer.

3 Melt 30g (1oz) chocolate (see page 44) and spread over the underside of each cap. Push the stalks, point first, into the holes. Leave on their sides until set.

Fruit Preparations

The addition of fruit often enriches the quality of a cake. The zest of sharp, citric lemons and oranges enhances the flavour, and adds a fine aroma and colour. Fruit-preserve glazes, richly sweet and yet tart, have a sticky texture that helps to bond the surface and add taste, as well as giving a glistening sheen to fresh fruit toppings. Cooked fruit lends moisture to drier cake mixtures.

COARSE LEMON ZEST

Drag a citrus zester (see page 39) firmly across the outside of a scrubbed or unwaxed lemon, taking care not to remove any of the bitter white pith that lies just underneath.

FINE LEMON SHREDS

Remove the zest from a lemon in strips using a peeler, taking care not to remove any pith. Cut into fine shreds. Blanch in boiling water for 30 seconds. Drain, refresh in cold water and drain again.

RASPBERRY SAUCE

Put 250g (8oz) raspberries and 2 tablespoons of icing sugar into a bowl. Crush into a purée. Press through a sieve and then chill.

Sieve the raspberries to remove the seeds

APPLE PUREE

Cook 250g (8oz) peeled, cored and sliced cooking apples with 60g (2oz) brown sugar and 1 tablespoon of water. Cook for 10–15 minutes until soft. Push through a sieve, cover and leave to cool.

PUMPKIN PUREE

Cut 1kg (2lb) fresh pumpkin into wedges. Peel and scoop out the seeds. Put into a steamer or colander resting over a pan of simmering water. Steam for 15–20 minutes until soft. Cool slightly, then push through a fine sieve. Cover and leave until cold.

REDCURRANT GLAZE

Put 3–4 tablespoons of redcurrant jelly and 2–3 teaspoons of water or Kirsch into a small pan and leave over a low heat until the jelly has melted and is completely clear. Cool until slightly thickened but use while still warm. This glaze covers a 23cm (9in) fruit flan.

APRICOT GLAZE

Put 125g (4oz) apricot jam and 3 tablespoons of water into a small pan and leave over a gentle heat until the jam has melted. Pour into a sieve over a small bowl and press through with a wooden spoon. Keeps in the refrigerator, in a sterilized screw-top jar, for 2 weeks. Warm it before use.

Fillings, Icings & Toppings

The flavour of a cake is often enhanced by the addition of a light cream filling and a delicious decorative topping. Here are key recipes for creams, icings and toppings used throughout the book. Always allow plenty of time for their preparation as they often benefit from chilling before use. Remember to remove any rings before you work with marzipan and sugarpaste.

SIMPLE BUTTERCREAM

INGREDIENTS

125g (4oz) unsalted butter, softened

250g (8oz) icing sugar, sifted

1 tsp vanilla extract or other flavouring (optional)

1 tbsp cream or milk

Put the softened butter into a bowl and gradually beat in the icing sugar until the mixture is pale and creamy. Beat in the vanilla extract or other flavouring and the cream or milk to give the mixture a spreading consistency.

CHESTNUT BUTTERCREAM

INGREDIENTS

125g (4oz) unsalted butter, softened

60g (2oz) icing sugar, sifted

1 egg yolk

125g (4oz) unsweetened chestnut purée

1 tbsp dark rum

Beat the softened butter, icing sugar and egg yolk together until pale and fluffy. Then beat in the chestnut purée, a spoonful at a time. Mix in the rum. Chill for about 30 minutes before using.

CREAM CHEESE FROSTING

INGREDIENTS

125g (4oz) cream cheese

15g (½ oz) icing sugar, sifted

150ml (¼ pint) double cream, chilled

Beat together the cheese and icing sugar until smooth. Gradually beat in all but 1½ tablespoons of the cream until the mixture reaches a soft dropping consistency. Do not overbeat: the frosting thickens as you spread it. Thin down with the remaining cream if necessary.

MOUSSELINE BUTTERCREAM

This is a firm, smooth buttercream that holds its shape even in warm conditions. To make sure it spreads smoothly, bring back to room temperature before using.

INGREDIENTS

75g (2½ oz) granulated sugar

3 egg yolks

180g (6oz) unsalted butter, softened

1 tsp vanilla extract

— HANDY TIPS —

◆ *The egg yolk mixture must be cool before it is added to the butter or the butter will melt.*

◆ *This buttercream will keep refrigerated for 4–5 days, or can be frozen for up to 1 month.*

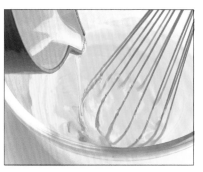

1 Gently heat the granulated sugar and 4 tablespoons of cold water in a small heavy-based pan until dissolved. Bring to the boil and boil to the soft ball stage at 115°C (240°F) (see page 153).

2 In another bowl, lightly whisk the egg yolks. Gradually pour in the hot syrup, whisking vigorously all the time. Continue whisking for about 5 minutes, until the mixture is pale, thick and cool.

3 Beat the butter until pale and creamy. Gradually beat in spoonfuls of the cooled egg and sugar mixture. Beat in the vanilla extract. Chill in the refrigerator for at least 30 minutes.

VARIATIONS
Coffee: Dissolve 2 tbsp instant coffee powder in 1 tbsp boiling water. Cool, then beat into the basic mixture.

Chocolate: Melt 100g (3½ oz) plain chocolate. Leave to cool, then beat in.
Liqueur: Beat in 1–2 tbsp dark rum, Kirsch, Grand Marnier or Cointreau.

Lemon: Beat in 1 tbsp lemon juice and the finely grated zest of 1 lemon.
Orange: Beat in 1 tbsp orange juice and the finely grated zest of 1 orange.

CHOCOLATE GANACHE

This is a smooth, rich and quite delicious unsweetened chocolate cream. The ganache is cooked, and then cooled for 1–1½ hours, but must be used while still soft because it hardens once cold. For a fresh vanilla flavour, first infuse a 5cm (2in) piece of vanilla pod in the cream. Remove the pod before adding the grated chocolate. This quantity of ganache is sufficient to cover a 23cm (9in) cake.

INGREDIENTS

300ml (½ pint) double cream
75g (2½ oz) plain chocolate, finely grated

1 Pour the cream into a small pan and slowly bring to the boil over a gentle heat. Take the cream off the heat and gradually stir in the grated chocolate until well incorporated.

2 Leave to cool in the refrigerator until firm but not set. Beat well until the mixture is paler in colour.

— *HANDY TIP* —

♦ *In warm weather the chocolate quantity can be increased slightly to give a firmer set.*

QUICK CHOCOLATE BUTTERCREAM

INGREDIENTS

1 tsp instant coffee powder
1 tsp cocoa powder
60g (2oz) plain chocolate, broken into pieces
250g (8oz) unsalted butter, softened
75g (2½ oz) icing sugar, sifted

1 Dissolve the coffee and cocoa powder in 2 tablespoons of boiling water. Pour into a small heatproof bowl, add the chocolate pieces and melt over a small pan of simmering water, stirring occasionally. Leave to cool until thickened but not set.

2 In another bowl, beat the butter and icing sugar together until pale and fluffy. Add the chocolate and stir in until well combined. Then beat the mixture until it becomes pale, fluffy and thick. This will keep refrigerated in a sealed container for up to 1 week.

CREME PATISSIERE

Crème pâtissière, or pastry cream, is a rich, custard-like mixture used to fill sweet flans and pastries. It is much thicker than normal custard. This prevents the pastry base of fruit flans from becoming soggy and enables them to be sliced neatly. It can also be piped successfully.

— *HANDY TIPS* —

♦ *Crème pâtissière can be thinned down by folding in a little lightly whipped cream once it is cold if you wish.*

♦ *It will keep for up to 2 days in the refrigerator.*

INGREDIENTS

275ml (9fl oz) milk
¼ of a vanilla pod or ½ tsp vanilla extract
3 egg yolks
60g (2oz) caster sugar
15g (½ oz) plain flour
15g (½ oz) cornflour
3 tbsp double cream

1 Bring the milk to the boil in a small pan. If you are using a vanilla pod, add it to the milk and set aside for about 30 minutes to infuse.

2 Put the egg yolks into a small heatproof bowl. Add the sugar and beat until slightly pale and creamy. Sift the flour and cornflour over the egg yolk mixture and beat together well until the mixture becomes smooth.

3 Remove the vanilla pod and bring the milk back to the boil. Pour on to the egg yolk mixture and mix carefully. Return to the pan and bring to the boil, stirring vigorously. Simmer for 2 minutes, keeping stirring, until smooth and thick.

4 Stir in the vanilla extract, if using, and the cream. Pour into a bowl and press clingfilm or buttered greaseproof paper on to the surface. Leave to cool and then chill for 2 hours before using.

MARZIPAN

Use to cover celebration cakes and for smaller decorations. This recipe makes 500g (1lb), enough to cover an 18cm (7in) fruit cake.

INGREDIENTS

125g (4oz) icing sugar, sifted

125g (4oz) caster sugar

250g (8oz) ground almonds

1 tsp lemon juice

few drops of almond extract (optional)

2 egg whites

Mix the icing and caster sugars and almonds in a bowl. Add the lemon juice, almond extract and enough egg white to make a soft dough. Knead briefly on a surface dusted with icing sugar until smooth. Wrap in clingfilm until needed.

SUGARPASTE

Also known as fondant icing, this is used to decorate novelty cakes and wedding cakes. It is very simple to make and gives a wonderfully smooth, professional finish. This recipe makes 500g (1lb) sugarpaste, sufficient to cover a 20cm (8in) cake. To colour the icing, add very small quantities of powdered or paste food colouring, and knead in until it is evenly distributed throughout the sugarpaste.

INGREDIENTS

425g (14oz) icing sugar, sifted

1 egg white

1 tbsp liquid glucose

1 Sift the icing sugar into a bowl. Add the egg white and liquid glucose and gradually stir together with a small round-bladed knife until it starts to stick together in lumps. Knead the pieces together in the bowl to form a ball.

2 Turn the mixture out on to a surface dusted with icing sugar. Knead for about 10 minutes until the paste is very smooth, dusting the surface with more icing sugar to prevent it from sticking. Wrap tightly in clingfilm. Sugarpaste will keep in an airtight container in the refrigerator for a few weeks.

PROCESSOR METHOD
Sift the icing sugar into the bowl of a food processor. Add the egg white and liquid glucose and process until it forms a smooth ball. Knead gently to blend.

GLACE ICING

This simple icing is best on light textured cakes and pastries and is used while still warm. Iced cakes keep for only a few days before the icing starts to crack. The quantity here is sufficient to cover the top and sides of a 20–22cm (8–8½in) round cake.

INGREDIENTS

200g (7oz) icing sugar, sifted

7–8 tsp boiling water

4 drops of vanilla extract

1 Sift the icing sugar into a small bowl. Gradually stir in the boiling water until the mixture is smooth and coats the back of a spoon. If too thin, it will soak into the cake; if too thick, it will not spread. Adjust with icing sugar or water. Stir in the vanilla extract.

2 Rest the bowl over a small pan of simmering water and leave for 1–2 minutes until warm. Use immediately.

VARIATIONS
To colour the icing: Dip the tip of a fine skewer into liquid or paste food colouring. Stir in until evenly coloured.

To flavour the icing: Make as for the main recipe, omitting the vanilla extract and substituting the following liquids for the water:
Orange: 2 tbsp strained fresh orange juice and 1–2 tsp strained lemon juice.
Lemon: 7–8 tsp strained lemon juice.
Liqueur: 7–8 tsp spirit (such as dark rum, Cointreau, Kirsch).
Coffee: Dissolve 1 tbsp instant coffee powder in 1 tsp boiling water, plus 6–7 tsp additional boiling water.
Chocolate: Replace 30g (1oz) of the icing sugar with 30g (1oz) cocoa powder. Sift together then gradually add 7–8 tsp boiling water.

BOILED SUGAR SYRUP

When sugar and water are boiled a syrup forms. The more concentrated and hotter the syrup becomes, the darker and thicker it will be and the harder it will set. A "soft ball" syrup is used instead of sugar for making mousseline buttercream, and caramel can be used for decorating elaborate cakes. Adding cream of tartar prevents the syrup from crystallizing.

INGREDIENTS

pinch of cream of tartar

150ml (¼ pint) cold water

500g (1lb) granulated sugar

1 Mix the cream of tartar with 1 teaspoon of water. Pour the rest into a heavy-based pan. Tip the sugar into the centre and heat gently until the sugar has dissolved and the liquid is clear.

2 Stir in the dissolved cream of tartar. Increase the heat and bring to the boil. Stand the sugar thermometer in the pan and boil rapidly to the required temperature (see above).

SIMPLE SUGAR SYRUP

This is a basic stock syrup that can be made in advance and stored in the refrigerator as a base for flavoured syrups to moisten layered cakes.

INGREDIENTS

125ml (4fl oz) water

200g (7oz) granulated or caster sugar

3 Take the pan off the heat and plunge the base into cold water to stop the syrup cooking further. Use straight away.

Soft Ball: Boil the syrup for about 1 minute until it reaches 115°C (240°F). If you drop a little of the syrup into a glass of cold water, then knead it between your fingers, it should form a soft ball.

Caramel: Boil the syrup for about 7 minutes until it reaches 173°C (345°F) and turns a rich amber colour. Be careful; if cooked for too long it will burn.

Warm the sugar thermometer before using

Do not stir the sugar syrup at all during boiling

Place the water and sugar in a heavy-based pan. Leave over a low heat, stirring constantly, until the sugar has completely dissolved and the liquid is clear. Bring the liquid to a rolling boil and immediately remove the pan from the heat. Leave the syrup until absolutely cold and then pour it into a sterilized jar and seal well. Keep refrigerated until needed; it will keep almost indefinitely.

VARIATIONS
Liqueur syrup: Mix 1 tbsp Cointreau, Grand Marnier, dark rum, Tia Maria or Kirsch with 2 tbsp syrup.
Rum and citrus syrup: Stir ½ tsp each of finely grated orange and lemon zest into 6 tbsp warm syrup. Leave for 10 minutes. Strain and mix with 3 tbsp dark rum.
Coffee syrup: Dissolve 1 tbsp instant coffee powder in 1 tsp boiling water. Cool and mix with 1 tbsp syrup.

What Went Wrong?

WHISKED & SEPARATED EGG MIXTURES

Why is the cake's texture dense and heavy?

- The eggs were too small.
- Insufficient air was whisked into the egg and sugar mixture.
- The flour was not folded in gently by hand using a large metal spoon.
- The melted butter was too hot when added, causing it to sink down through the whisked foam.
- The oven temperature was too low.

Why has the top of the cake dropped?

- The oven temperature was too hot.
- The cake was not cooked for long enough.
- The cake tin was knocked during baking.
- The oven door was opened too soon which created a draught.

Why did the Swiss roll crack while being rolled?

- The sponge was overcooked so it was too dry.
- The mixture was not spread out evenly in the baking tray, causing some parts to overcook and dry out before the rest of the sponge was done.
- The crisp edges of the cooked sponge were not trimmed away before rolling.
- The sponge was left for too long before rolling.

BLENDED & CREAMED MIXTURES

Why has the mixture curdled?

- The ingredients were not at room temperature.
- The butter and sugar were not creamed together well enough before adding the eggs.
- The eggs were added too quickly.

Why is the cake's texture heavy?

- The butter, sugar and eggs were not beaten together for long enough.
- The flour was stirred in too vigorously, therefore knocking out the air incorporated during creaming.
- Too much flour was added to the creamed mixture.

- The baking powder was left out.
- The oven temperature was not hot enough.

Why has the cake peaked and cracked?

- The oven temperature was too hot, causing the outside of the cake to bake and form a crust too quickly. As the mixture in the centre of the cake continued to cook and rise, it burst up through the top of the cake.
- The cake was on too high a shelf in the oven.

Why has the dried fruit sunk in the cake?

- The pieces of fruit were too large and too heavy.
- The sugary syrup on the outside of the glacé fruit was not washed off, causing them to slide through the mixture as it heated.
- The washed and dried fruit was not dusted with flour before being added to the mixture.
- The cake mixture was over-beaten or too slack so it could not hold the fruit in place.
- The oven temperature was too low, causing the mixture to melt before it set to hold the fruit in place.

GENERAL

Why did the cake rise unevenly in the oven?

- The flour was not blended sufficiently into the main mixture.
- The sides of the tin were unevenly greased.
- The temperature inside the oven was uneven.
- The oven temperature was too high.

Why did the mixture overflow in the oven?

- The size of the cake tin recommended in the recipe was not used. The uncooked mixture should fill the tin by no more than two thirds.

Why was the cake overcooked and the top burned?

- All the recipes in the book have been baked in a conventional oven. Fan-assisted ovens bake more quickly so the temperature will need to be adjusted. Refer to the manufacturer's handbook.

► Rich fruit cakes usually require longer baking so they should be covered with foil half-way through.

Why was the cake burned on the bottom?

► A poor quality tin was used. If too thin, a tin can develop hot spots and warp in the oven.
► The cake was baked near to the bottom of the oven.

Why are there holes in the baked cake?

► The tin with the raw whisked cake mixture was not rapped on the work surface before baking.

Why did small brown speckles appear on the surface of the cake or biscuits?

► Granulated sugar was used instead of caster sugar. This is too coarse and does not dissolve as easily.

PASTRY

Why did the pastry shrink away from the sides of the flan tin during baking?

► The pastry was stretched while being rolled out.
► The pastry was not allowed to rest before and after being rolled out. This helps it to lose its elasticity before being baked.

Why was the pastry hard and tough?

► The raw pastry was over-mixed in the bowl or kneaded too much.
► Too much liquid was added to the rubbed-in flour and butter mixture.
► Too much flour was used for dusting the work surface when rolling out.

Why was the base of the flan soggy?

► The cooked pastry shell was not brushed with beaten egg white while still hot.
► The cooled pastry case was not brushed with a thin layer of apricot glaze before adding the filling.

CHOUX PASTRY

Why did the pastry collapse as soon as it was removed from the oven?

► Plain flour was used instead of strong plain flour.
► The pastry was not baked for long enough.

► A hole was not pierced through the base of the cooked pastry. The trapped steam caused the pastry to go soft again.
► The oven temperature was too high.

MERINGUES

Why did the egg whites take so long to whisk?

► The egg whites were too cold. They must be at room temperature before whisking.
► The bowl or whisk was slightly greasy. Both must be spotlessly clean.
► The eggs were not fresh.
► A little of the egg yolk was dropped into the egg whites during separation. The fat in the yolk inhibited the egg whites from producing a good foam.
► The whites were not lifted up high during whisking. This helps to form a good airy structure.

Why did a clear syrup run out of the meringues during baking?

► Granulated sugar was used. It is too coarse and does not dissolve in the mixture like caster sugar.
► The sugar was added too quickly or too much at once so that it did not have time to dissolve.
► There might have been some form of moisture present in the oven during baking.
► The meringue was not baked immediately.

Why were the meringues still moist in the middle after baking?

► They were not baked and allowed to dry out in the oven for long enough.

CREAMS, ICINGS & FILLINGS

Why was it difficult to whip the cream into peaks?

► The cream and whisk were not chilled before use.
► The cream was not fresh.
► The wrong type of cream was used.

Why did the icing or cream have lumps of icing sugar in it?

► The icing sugar was not sifted before it was added. Lumps of icing sugar never disperse once they are mixed with the other ingredients.

Templates

Use these templates to help you decorate the Teddy Bear Cake (see page 136 for the recipe). Carefully trace the teddy bear and the number appropriate to the age of the child on to a sheet of tracing or silicone paper. Then cut them out and use as described in the recipe.

Index

Acknowledgments

Author's Appreciation
I would like to thank the many people who have been involved in putting this book together. The team at Dorling Kindersley has worked long and hard over many months. I thank Debbie Major and Carolyn Ryden, my project editor and senior editor, for coping with my text; Jo Grey for her fine artwork and selective eye; Susannah Marriott, whose inspiration this book was, and Carole Ash, who had the vision. I enjoyed working with them all. It was good to see my recipes prepared so beautifully for photography by Janice Murfitt and Angela Kingsbury; and to work with Dave King, who took such wonderful photographs despite the highest summer temperatures imaginable. I wish to acknowledge with gratitude my good friends Lynda Dyer and Joanne Hill, who helped me prepare and test the many recipes, and Virginia Owen, who spent many long hours with me in my kitchen. I especially wish to thank Valerie Barrett for her support in working out recipe problems and exhaustive testing. I thank my friend Hans van den Klinkenberg, Swiss Chef Pâtissier who allowed me to use two of his recipes. Lastly but not least I must acknowledge the various cookery writers from around the world in centuries past, whose books inspired me to write in the first instance.

Dorling Kindersley would like to thank Catherine Atkinson for preparing some of the cakes that appear in the book; Nasim Mawji, Claire Benson and Jackie Jackson for editorial assistance; Vanessa Courtier for initial design work; Annette O'Sullivan and Kate L Scott for design assistance; and Gilly Newman for illustrations.

Picture Credits : Key to pictures: t=top; c=centre; b=bottom; l=left; r=right
Photography by Dave King except: Martin Cameron 30–1, 32–3, 34–5, 36–7, 38–9, 40–1; Terry McCormick 11, 13cr, 13br, 21, 75, 114, 128–9; Andy Crawford 41t, 145cr, 145cr, 145br; Steve Gorton 32tr, 32cr, 32br; The Bridgeman Art Library 6–7; Mary Evans Picture Library 8; The Hulton Deutsch Collection 6bl.

Mail Order Addresses for Baking Equipment
Lakeland Plastics: Alexandra Buildings, Windermere, Cumbria LA23 1BQ. Tel: 015394 88100
Divertimenti: Mail Order Dept, P.O. Box 6611, London SW6 6XU. Tel: 0171 386 9911
David Mellor: Mail Order Dept, 4 Sloane Square, London SW1 8EE. Tel: 0171 730 4259